6 Principles for Teaching English Language Learners in All Classrooms

D1406614

We dedicate this book to the caring teachers in schools across the United States who strive to work effectively in supporting English language learners. We also dedicate it to the many immigrant children and their families who strive for a better life and often face many challenges in the process.

6 Principles for Teaching English Language Learners in All Classrooms

Ellen McIntyre | Diane W. Kyle | Cheng-Ting Chen
Jayne Kraemer | Johanna Parr

CORWIN PRESS
A SAGE Company

Copyright © 2009 by Corwin Press

All rights reserved. When forms and sample documents are included, their use is authorized only by educators, local school sites, and/or noncommercial or nonprofit entities who have purchased the book. Except for that usage, no part of this book may be reproduced or utilized in any form or by any means, electronic or mechanical, including photocopying, recording, or by any information storage and retrieval system, without permission in writing from the publisher.

For information:

Corwin Press
A SAGE Company
2455 Teller Road
Thousand Oaks, California 91320
www.corwinpress.com

SAGE Ltd.
1 Oliver's Yard
55 City Road
London, EC1Y 1SP
United Kingdom

SAGE India Pvt. Ltd.
B 1/I 1 Mohan Cooperative
Industrial Area
Mathura Road, New Delhi 110 044
India

SAGE Asia-Pacific Pte. Ltd.
33 Pekin Street #02-01
Far East Square
Singapore 048763

Printed in the United States of America

Library of Congress Cataloging-in-Publication Data
Six principles for teaching English language learners in all classrooms
/ Ellen McIntyre ... [et al.].
    p. cm.
 Includes bibliographical references and index.
 ISBN 978-1-4129-5833-2 (cloth : acid-free paper) — ISBN
978-1-4129-5834-9 (pbk. : acid-free paper)
1. English language—Study and teaching—Foreign speakers.
I. McIntyre, Ellen. II. Title.

PE1128.A2S592 2009
428.2′4—dc22

2008008418

This book is printed on acid-free paper.

08 09 10 11 10 9 8 7 6 5 4 3 2 1

Acquisitions Editor: Dan Alpert
Associate Editor: Megan Bedell
Production Editor: Appingo Publishing Services
Cover Designer: Lisa Miller
Graphic Designer: Scott Van Atta

Contents

Preface

Today's U.S. schools are becoming wonderfully diverse, with students from a variety of language backgrounds entering our classrooms each year. In the midst of this diversity, we, as teachers, are challenged to provide these students with the academic skills they need to be successful. Some of these students are recent immigrants who are just beginning to acquire English, while others have lived in the United States for longer periods of time. One thing certain to us and to many other educators who work to improve the academic opportunities for English language learners (ELLs) is that these students and their families value education, want to learn, and are capable of success when given the right kind of support.

In the midst of the current political scene of 2008, heated by debates on closing borders, deporting undocumented immigrants, and creating new policies for schooling immigrants, teachers across the country are going about the business of teaching the diverse population of students in their classrooms. We have struggled as we have searched to find an instructional model most appropriate for our ELLs. We wanted a model grounded in the theory and research on effective practice in teaching ELLs, one that was academically rigorous and that honored the successful strategies we were already using in our classrooms while adding to our repertoire. Like many educators, we wanted a model that reflects the rich and complex nature of teaching and learning and has been shown to be effective for all students. We also wanted a flexible and practical model. This book is a result of our goals and efforts to help our own practices and to provide guidance for other teachers facing the same challenges.

This is a book written for both elementary and middle school teachers. Although it will provide help for specialist ELL teachers, we particularly address the needs of the regular classroom teacher who may not have had extensive training in teaching English language learners. These teachers are essential for the success of our immigrant and English-learning population. Our motivation in writing this book is our belief that all English language learners should have the opportunity to learn academic content such as biology and forms of poetry simultaneously while learning English. However, we realize that most teachers have not learned how to address both content and language development in a regular classroom. Furthermore, most mainstream teachers have not learned how to extend the curriculum they are required to teach to include the lives of their students, although research shows that such connections can assist in students' academic understandings.

This book presents a model of instruction based on decades of research on effective instruction of diverse populations, including—especially—English language learners. The model is grounded in the Vygotskian (Vygotsky, 1978) teaching-learning framework that takes into consideration students' culture, history, language, and learning patterns. The "Six Principles" model involves five standards of effective pedagogy derived from multiple studies through the Center for Research on Education, Diversity, and Excellence (CREDE) and family involvement, a key to the academic success of any student.

The CREDE standards for pedagogy include (1) *Joint Productive Activity* (teachers and students work together on joint products), (2) *Language Learning* across the curriculum (teachers help students apply literacy strategies and language competence in all areas of the curriculum), (3) *Contextualization* (teachers connect instruction to students' experiences), (4) *Rigorous Curriculum* (teachers design instruction to advance understanding at complex levels), and (5) *Instructional Conversation* (teachers provide instruction in small groups using academic dialogue as a tool for learning). These five standards cross curricular areas and age groups and work in concert. The sixth "principle" of this model is family involvement, presented as a way to help students connect their prior experience and knowledge with academic content.

This book is organized around each of the "principles," which include the five standards of pedagogy and family involvement. Each chapter focuses specifically on one of these principles, although all are richly illustrated in vignettes, lessons, tips, and even dialogue, all captured through observation and videotape. The examples come from real classrooms of elementary and middle school teachers who have been trained in the model. Each lesson or vignette is followed by a description of how the lesson exemplifies the model. We use CREDE's "indicators" of each standard—pointers for monitoring your own implementation of the standard—to examine the lessons we share. The extra strategies and tips help make the model work in all kinds of classrooms—from elementary to middle grades, and from mainstream to self-contained ESL classrooms.

In a recent interview conducted with English language learners in the classroom of a teacher identified as highly effective, we asked the students what their teacher did specifically that helped them learn. The students eagerly provided many examples, such as research projects that provided a way to share about their home countries and things they knew, opportunities to work together to help one another learn, the extensive use of supplementary materials, and much support when needed. As one student said, "Some teachers explain us only a little...or really fast...but [their teacher] explain us like with the time that we need and with easy words."

The students didn't use the terms of "contextualization" or "joint productive activity" or "rigorous curriculum," and they didn't refer to the importance of scaffolding students as they stretched toward new understandings. But, they implicitly knew what kinds of teaching helped them learn best. The principles explained and illustrated throughout this book will benefit not only the English language learners in U.S. classrooms but also, ultimately, all learners. They are the essence of what good teaching is all about.

Acknowledgments

We have been fortunate in the past few years to work with classroom teachers, school district leaders, and other members of the community who are dedicated to working both with immigrant and refugee families new to the United States and with other students still learning English. Our particular focus has been on supporting the academic success of the many English language learners entering public school classrooms. We are grateful for the funding provided by the U. S. Department of Education's Office of English Language Acquisition and for the interest of our project director, Rebecca Richey. The funding made it possible to conduct a three-year professional development project with K–12 classroom teachers on how to work effectively with English language learners and their families. We learned a great deal from the experience and acknowledge with thanks the participants, our leadership team of ESL instructional coaches—Scott Beldon, Vongmany Edmonds, Angie Reimer, and Maria Scherrer—and current and former ESL coordinators—Marti Kinny, Berta Calvert, and Maxine Elliott.

We are also grateful for the teachers who provided examples from their classrooms to use in this book— Lisa Allen from Appingo, Carmen Cripps, Georgia Drury, Erin Forman, Mary Hall, Cori Loew, Linda McAvinue, Gayle Moore, Justin Patton, Iraida Villar, and Vickie Wheatley. We know that those reading will appreciate the real experiences of other teachers.

This is our third book published with Corwin Press, and we continue to appreciate the enthusiastic support and helpful guidance throughout the process. We especially thank our former editor, Rachel Livsey, our new editor, Dan Alpert, and the reviewers who offered useful suggestions. We thank as well April Bowling of North Carolina State University for her assistance with the final book preparation.

Authors' note: The work that led to the writing of this article was supported by the U.S. Department of Education, PR Award Number T195N040101. The contents, findings, and opinions expressed here are those of the authors and do not necessarily represent the positions or policies of the U.S. Department of Education.

Publisher's Acknowledgments

Corwin Press gratefully acknowledges the contributions of the following reviewers:

Carol Gallegos
Literacy Coach
Hanford Elementary School District
Hanford, CA

Gladys M. González
ELL Teacher
Whittier Elementary School
Boise, ID

Xiadong Niu
ELL Teacher
Forest Hills, NY

Jorge P. Osterling
Associate Professor of Education
College of Education and Human Development
Fairfax, VA

Oneyda M. Paneque
Assistant Professor
Miami Dade College School of Education
Miami, FL

Patricia B. Schwartz
Principal
Thomas Jefferson Middle School
Teaneck, NJ

About the Authors

 **Ellen McIntyre** is a professor and Head of Elementary Education at North Carolina State University. She has codirected grant projects funded by the Center for Research on Education, Diversity, and Excellence (CREDE) and, most recently, she directed a project on "Sheltered instruction and family involvement: An approach to raising achievement of LEP students," funded by the U.S. Department of Education. Her research has focused entirely on populations of students who have historically been disenfranchised from schools: students of poverty, minorities, struggling readers, and English language learners. Ellen frames her work within a sociocultural perspective on teaching and learning, which grounds how she examines teaching, student engagement, and achievement. She has also been a language learner herself; for the last several years, she has worked diligently on learning Spanish.

 **Diane Kyle** is a professor of curriculum in the Department of Teaching and Learning at the University of Louisville. She codirected, with Ellen McIntyre, the grant projects funded by the Center for Research on Education, Diversity, and Excellence and the U. S. Department of Education. These projects have led to several articles, presentations, and books on effective instructional strategies, family engagement efforts, and teacher reflection and change. In addition to teaching a graduate course on strategies for teaching English language learners, she tutors in the schools with recent immigrant students who are learning English.

Cheng-Ting Chen is from Taiwan and has studied and worked in the United States for seven years. After receiving her Master's degree from Western Kentucky University, she taught ESL reading and writing classes at Atherton High School in Jefferson County (KY) Public Schools. She is currently working on her doctoral program at the University of Louisville, focusing on ESL literacy with the goal of improving the English education programs in Taiwan.

Jayne Kramer is a teacher with Jefferson County Public Schools in Louisville, Kentucky, teaching Language Arts to middle school English language learners. In addition to her English/Language Arts certification, she holds an endorsement to teach Reading and Writing in grades K–12, as well as an endorsement to teach English as a Second Language. Prior to teaching middle school, she taught high school English language learners and has also worked as an ESL instructional coach within the Jefferson County school district. She is currently in the process of completing her doctoral program at the University of Louisville, focusing on new literacies and English language learners.

Johanna Robinson Parr is a teacher at Klondike Elementary, a Jefferson County Public School located in Louisville, Kentucky. She earned her Bachelor's degree in education at Western Kentucky University and her Master's degree in education at Indiana University. She has taught kindergarten for several years. Her first JCPS appointment was within a school with 95% economically disadvantaged, at-risk minority students. After years of working with socioeconomically disadvantaged students, Parr transferred to her present teaching position, where she specializes in addressing the needs of ESL students. Parr has used her diversified teaching background to offer a broad view on the needs of ESL students and the methods and nurturing that ensure success for this student population.

1

Introduction

In recent years, we have seen our country become more culturally, ethnically, and linguistically diverse. It is not unusual for schools in the United States to have more than 20 different languages spoken by the students; in some schools, that number is over 100! As a result, schools have scrambled to meet students' needs by offering English as a Second Language (ESL) programs, bilingual programs, and immersion programs. This attention to the immigrant child and other English language learners has helped many children, but not enough of them. Because the immigrant population continues to increase, a well-designed curricular and instructional model in mainstream classrooms that can assist English language learners (ELLs) alongside their native English peers is crucial.

We believe that in today's schools, all teachers can and must see themselves as teachers of English language learners. In past years, when immigrant students entered a school, they were often "turfed" to a specialist—sometimes to an ESL teacher, if the school was lucky enough to have one with the required certificate, but often simply to a special education class. At times, the students were left to sink or swim on their own, and they often sank. Today, with so many English language learners in schools, providing specialist programs for them is unrealistic and sometimes detrimental to their academic development because they miss out on valuable opportunities to learn content. Instead, through particular instructional principles, teachers of all grade levels and subject areas must learn to adapt their teaching to be more inclusive and more effective.

The mainstream classroom teacher is essential for the success of our immigrant population. All students should have the opportunity to learn content such as chemistry, algebra, and geography while simultaneously learning English. Yet, most regular classroom teachers have not learned how to address the needs of English language learners in their instructional plans and activities so that the students learn the content and simultaneously improve their English. In fact, immigrants and other ELLs most often need help with the academic language (the language of the discipline). Many immigrant students who have been in the United States more than three years, as well as some native-born children with foreign-language-speaking parents, sound comfortable with English and can converse fluently with friends. Yet, their abilities may be deceiving, as these students may still be unfamiliar with academic language and all its complexities.

English Language Learners of All Kinds

It is easy to think of all English language learners as similar—they all need to learn English, don't they? The reality is that different groups of ELLs bring to the classroom subtle but significant differences in their knowledge and skills (Freeman & Freeman, 2002). Some students, although newly arrived in the United States, have received adequate schooling in their native country. These students often make quick progress academically, although they still need support to learn the language. But even these students might struggle when faced with standardized tests in English. Being part of the regular classroom provides these students with a learning context in which they can make the important connections between academic areas of knowledge in their first and subsequent languages.

Other immigrant students in our classrooms may have had little or no formal schooling in their native country. These students not only face the challenge of learning English, but they also need to learn the academic strategies and skills necessary to become successful students. They cannot rely on a foundation of academic skills or content knowledge in their native language, and they may struggle not only with standardized tests but also with the everyday coursework and experiences of an American classroom. For these students, being part of the regular classroom allows them the opportunity to absorb the school culture and academic routines that they have been missing.

A third but often overlooked group of ELLs is those who have been in the United States several years but are still faltering academically. These students often have native-like oral language fluency, but because they have missed school for long periods of time, or because they have not had a consistent program of instruction, they have huge gaps in their learning. These students may receive adequate grades because they do their work, yet, while teachers often want to pass them on to the next grade level, these students may not be learning all they need to prepare them for college or work outside of high school. They also will likely struggle to pass standardized tests, which often reveal that they are not on grade level, especially in the areas of reading and mathematics (Freeman & Freeman, 2002).

Finally, there are many children who were born in the United States and have a strong command of conversational English but who have foreign-born parents who speak a language other than English at home. While these children are lucky to be able to learn two languages from birth, there still may be some gaps in language learning and content learning that may be missed.

While these groups of English language learners vary in what they bring with them to the classroom, they do have one thing in common. All groups may be in danger of academic failure due in part to how schools attend or do not attend to these students. In this world of high-stakes testing and accountability, pulling any or all of these different types of ELLs from the regular classroom in order to teach them English may be a disservice when they so obviously need the rich content that the regular classroom teacher provides. Of course, if mainstream teachers are doing little to help them, the students might be better off in self-contained classrooms.

Language Learning: How Does It Happen?

The theory behind language acquisition further supports the point that ELLs acquire language best when they are part of the regular classroom. First, we must differentiate between language *acquisition* and language *learning* (Krashen, 1990). To fully understand the difference, we can think back on our own experiences in learning a foreign language in high school or college. For example, as students in a Spanish-as-a-foreign-language class, we were required to learn about Spanish grammar, Spanish vocabulary, and even various Hispanic cultural norms, but most of us never acquired Spanish to any level of fluency. We learned about the Spanish language, but we rarely had the opportunity to use it in authentic communicative situations. Plunk us down in the middle of Mexico and, even after four years or more of traditional language study, we will more than likely struggle to put together the most basic of sentences. Why? Because acquiring a language is in part a subconscious process that occurs when the learner uses the language to communicate. The advantage of teaching ELLs in the regular classroom is that they are naturally immersed in the work of communicating for authentic purposes. Rather than focusing only on learning English, they're focused on learning the content while acquiring English at the same time.

While this theory of language acquisition does make sense, many educators still think of language learning as studying the rules of grammar. Language acquisition theorist Stephen Krashen (1990) argues that the purpose of consciously learning the rules of a language is not to acquire the language but to *monitor* its use. He further notes that three almost impossible conditions must be met in order for speakers to monitor their language use effectively. First, they must have an adequate amount of time to process the language they hear. Second, they must be able to focus on form in order to produce a correct response. And third, they must know the rules of the grammar precisely in order to form that correct response. In the normal flow of a conversation, or in the midst of a classroom environment, none of these conditions can be met. In fact, students rarely use their conscious grammar knowledge on anything but a grammar test.

The natural order to language acquisition cannot be circumvented through learning language rules. Just as young children who are learning to speak acquire grammatical structures in a natural order, so does anyone learning a new language (Krashen, 1990). Students learn when the language they hear and process is *one step beyond* their current comprehension level. When students are placed in situations that require authentic communication (e.g., the regular content area classroom) and they can follow the general flow of a discussion, they are naturally challenged to reach out and grasp the meaning of what is just a bit beyond their comprehension level. Krashen calls this the "Input Hypothesis" and explains that this is a critical condition for language acquisition. If an acquirer is at a stage of level i, the input he or she should be exposed to (and potentially understand) should contain $i + 1$ (Krashen, 1990). This concept reflects Vygotsky's (1978) zone of proximal development, defined as the distance between a child's actual cognitive capacity and the level of potential development. Thus, it is natural for students of diverse experiences and language proficiency to participate in the same classroom lessons. They will "take from," or acquire, the language for which they are developmentally ready.

It may also be helpful to be familiar with the common stages of second language development. Corder (1973) and Brown (2000) propose the "PEPSI" model to explain these stages. They divide the process of second language acquisition into four stages, or levels: "Pre-Production Stage," "Early Production Stage," "Emergent Stage," and "Intermediate Fluency Stage."

Table 1.1 Summary of Corder and Brown's Stages of Language Development

Level 1	**Pre-Production Stage (Silent Period):** Minimal comprehension; no verbal production.
Level 2	**Early Production Stage:** Limited comprehension; one- or two-word response; random errors.
Level 3	**Emergent Stage:** Increased comprehension; simple sentences; unable to correct errors; possible "backsliding."
Level 4	**Intermediate Fluency Stage:** Very good comprehension; more complex sentences; complex errors in speech; able to correct errors when they are pointed out.
Level 5	**Stabilization Stage:** No problem with fluency and intended meanings; able to self-correct errors; possible "fossilization."

According to the above chart, teachers who have newly arrived students should anticipate a "Silent Period" during which students may not be able to (or know how to) respond. How long each stage may last depends on an individual student's specific situation. For example, the silent period could last from one month to even a year. Gradually, ELLs become more capable of daily conversations. However, language learners commonly "backslide" during certain periods or when they reach a bottleneck. Furthermore, even when English language learners reach the Stabilization Stage, they could face a phenomenon known as *fossilization*, meaning they carry their

L1 (first language) rules, systems, pronunciation, and so on into their L2 (second language). Having an accent illustrates one obvious example of fossilization.

BICS and CALP

These two acronyms, BICS and CALP (Cummins, 1979), help clarify the kinds of language expertise ELLs need to acquire. BICS, Basic Interpersonal Communicative Skills, refers to the oral language we use in our daily encounters with others, such as family, friends, clerks, and others with whom we have casual conversation. Immigrants first learn these language skills when they arrive in the United States, and depending on opportunities and necessities, some learn these quickly and soon sound like fluent speakers of English. However, as important as BICS is, success in school requires more.

Students must also obtain CALP, or Cognitive Academic Language Proficiency. This is the language of the discipline—vocabulary and usage distinct by subject areas. CALP includes words like *diameter, radius,* and *circumference* that all students need to learn geometry, but it also includes more common words like *figure* and *space* that may confuse an English language learner who has learned different meanings for these words. All fields have specialized language, including English language arts (e.g., *prose, genre,* or *meter* and *line* in poetry), that is critical for academic success.

Cummins (2003) explains that "the distinction [between BICS and CALP] was intended to draw attention to the very different time periods typically required by immigrant children to acquire conversational fluency in their second language as compared to grade-appropriate academic proficiency in that language" (p. 322). He suggests that, on average, students can acquire conversational fluency at a functional level within about two years, but academic language proficiency takes five to seven years to acquire. If we hear students speak English fluently, but know they still struggle academically, a good reason for this may be students' lack of academic language.

Many English language learners exit from language support programs after one to two years, possibly because they sound fluent and their teachers assume they are ready for the mainstream classroom. But if they have not been in classrooms in which they learn both content concepts and language skills, they may not be as academically ready as once thought, due to a lack of academic language. Clearly, knowing how to teach ELLs is an issue not only for ESL teachers but also for regular, or mainstream, classroom teachers.

All Teachers as Teachers of English Language Learners

Teachers who are prepared to teach ELLs in special programs, most often called "ESL programs" in U.S. colleges and universities, usually have a deep linguistic and cultural understanding of various ELL groups, and many have a wide repertoire of instructional strategies. Ideally, schools will have one or more prepared teachers in each school serving large populations of English learners. Jayne Kraemer, one of the authors of this book, is such a teacher. Yet, because of the rapid increase in immigration into the United States, we cannot and should not rely on ESL-trained teachers.

Indeed, you don't have to be a trained ESL teacher to help English language learners. Except for their language and cultural background, these students are the same as other students in regular classrooms. You might have students with different learning styles, religions, socioeconomic conditions, personalities, attitudes, interests, and talents that require you to think of various strategies to better support their individual needs. ELLs can be considered similarly. Just as we would not depend on one strategy to teach all students, in light of their diverse needs, neither would we choose one way to support ELLs. In contrast, we need to observe them carefully to know their strengths and weaknesses and then figure out how to provide the assistance they need. As Krashen (1981) noted,

> The best methods are therefore those that supply 'comprehensible input' in low anxiety situations, containing messages that students really want to hear. These methods do not force early production in the second language, but allow students to produce when they are 'ready,' recognizing that improvement comes from supplying communicative and comprehensible input, and not from forcing and correcting production (pp. 6–7).

Throughout this book, you will find detailed descriptions of useful strategies tried out in authentic classrooms by teachers working with English language learners. They build from research-based models and are ready for you to consider and adapt in your own settings.

A Look Back Is a Look Forward

Looking back at the language teaching methods that were once popular provides a foundation for understanding current language-teaching contexts, including the model we propose. It is not surprising to see traces of old pedagogies in new models. For example, the Grammar Translation Method dominated the language-teaching field during the late nineteenth century, and vestiges of it continue today. In this method, the language is taught in the students' mother tongue, rather than through the targeted language. The focus is on learning vocabulary and grammar, with little attention to real conversation. Not surprisingly, this method produces learners who, like the earlier example of the student of Spanish, can cite rules of the new language but who cannot necessarily speak the language! The model we describe in this book ("Six Principles") borrows little from the Grammar Translation model, except perhaps to suggest what teachers might *avoid* doing.

The Direct Method was popular in Europe, but not in the United States, in the first part of the twentieth century. In this method, all instruction is conducted in the target language, as is done in many classrooms today. The focus is on oral communication, and grammar is taught inductively. While some of the processes of this method are aspects of our instructional model, the Direct Method often neglects the kind of *explicit* teaching needed for some learners.

In the late 1940s and 1950s, the Audiolingual Method (ALM) borrowed principles from the Direct Method. Also called the "Army Method" because it was used to train military personnel in foreign languages, it too focused on oral communication, with virtually none of the grammar found in the traditional methods. Teachers present all new material in dialogue form and use tapes, language labs, and visual aids. Students learn vocabulary in context. This method, however, is like the others in that language learning, not the learning of content, is the focus. In the model described in this book, the focus is on learning language while simultaneously learning the content of the disciplines.

In the early 1970s, teaching methodology became influenced by linguistic and psychological theory. Therefore, approaches and techniques that stressed the importance of self-esteem, of students cooperatively learning together, of developing individual strategies for success, and focusing on the communicative process in language learning have been created and applied due to the growing interest of psychology in interpersonal relationships, group work, and communicative competence. For example, one method, referred to as Suggestopedia (Lozanov, 1979), capitalized on relaxed states of mind for maximum retention of material. When Lozanov and his followers experimented with the presentation of vocabulary, readings, dialogue, role-play, drama, and a variety of other activities, classical music was played in the background and students sat in soft, comfortable seats. This method did not prove to be any more beneficial for language learning than other methods. However, students did report having high levels of confidence.

Today, ELLs are taught in a variety of ways (August & Shanahan, 2006a) in total immersion programs, bilingual programs, traditional ESL programs, and in newcomer schools for those who have recently arrived in the United States. In recent years, there has been increasing interest in educating ELLs in the mainstream classroom through sheltered instruction. Sheltered instruction is a means for making grade-level academic content (e.g., science, social studies, math) more accessible for ELLs while at the same time promoting their language and literacy development. In sheltered instruction, teachers highlight key language features and incorporate strategies that make the content comprehensible to students. It can extend the time students have for getting language support services while giving them a jump-start on the content they need to learn.

One popular model for sheltered instruction is the Sheltered Instruction Observation Protocol (SIOP), developed by researchers from the Center for Research on Education, Diversity, and Excellence (CREDE) in collaboration with the Center for Applied Linguistics (Echevarria, Vogt, & Short, 2004). Their model includes attention to eight components of instruction: Preparation, Building Background, Comprehensible Input, Strategies, Interaction, Lesson Delivery, Practice, and Review. Many of the teachers we feature in this book, including all the authors, have been trained in this model. It is theoretically aligned with the Six Principles model we describe in this book.

Overview of the Book

This book represents a culmination of a three-year professional development and research project. The project focused on mainstream teachers implementing sheltered instruction and family involvement. Various analyses were conducted to assess the level of implementation and the effects on student learning (McIntyre, Kyle, & Chen, 2007; McIntyre, Kyle, Munoz, Chen, & Beldon, 2008) and on family involvement of ELLs (Chen, Kyle, & McIntyre, 2008). We use real examples of lessons that came mostly from this research project, in which we used evaluation rubrics along with audio- and videotaping.

In Chapter 2, we present our model of instruction for English language learners, which borrows from many of the research-based and research-proven ideas of the past as well as current research and theory, particularly that coming from CREDE, mentioned above. For the most part, the model presented here came directly from the research we conducted ourselves. Thus, you may notice ideas from the models described above, and you will notice dramatic departures from these methods as well. The model we present is a comprehensive instructional plan designed to benefit all learners while simultaneously meeting the specific needs of ELLs in the regular classroom.

Chapters 3–7 focus on the CREDE standards. We combine the overlapping, synchronized standards of CREDE throughout the book, as described above and illustrated in Chapter 2. While all standards work in concert, we will devote one chapter to each standard in order to carefully delineate what it looks like in practice in a variety of classrooms. The examples make the application of the standards vivid and understandable for the reader. Within each chapter, we provide commentary about how these particular instructional decisions are good for ELLs as well as for all students, and we offer suggestions for those making such attempts in their own classrooms.

This book will also include a chapter (Chapter 8) on another issue many teachers and schools face in working with ELLs—how to work successfully with the families of these students. Schools already struggle with how to engage the families of all students, and engaging immigrant families presents an even more urgent and unique challenge. Yet, in our experience, the families of ELLs are often particularly eager to participate in schools activities and they are families dedicated to the educational success of their children.

Chapter 8 will include general suggestions about family engagement as well as specific strategies teachers have implemented and found useful. We provide several tools for making connections with families and for learning from them.

Finally, in Chapter 9 we reflect on the model and on teachers' development toward full implementation of it. We highlight what we view as keys to successful implementation and high engagement and achievement of students. As you read, ponder such questions as these: In what ways do these examples illustrate "good teaching"? Why would this type of instruction be particularly helpful for ELLs? What do I learn from these examples that will help me modify my own teaching? We also caution readers not to become overwhelmed by the expectations of this sort of teaching nor by the examples we provide. We believe that most teachers successful at implementing these standards have done so gradually, taking on one standard at a time.

Cast of Characters

To illustrate the concepts presented in a vivid and realistic way, throughout the book we use actual examples from the classrooms of several teachers who represent different grades, content areas, school districts, and student demographics. Many of the lessons we include were videotaped, and we transcribed them for exact teaching episodes. For other lessons, we took notes while observing. In one case, we included a written lesson plan. These "characters" include

- Cori, a seventh-grade social studies teacher in a highly diverse, urban district;
- Vickie, a seventh-grade language arts teacher in a less diverse, suburban district;
- Justin, a high school teacher in an urban mid-sized town;
- Linda, a fourth-grade teacher in a highly diverse, urban district;
- Georgia, a first- and second-grade teacher in a small town;
- Mary, a third-grade teacher in a diverse, suburban school district serving students from all socioeconomic groups;
- Gayle, a nongraded primary teacher in a small town;
- Erin, a fifth-grade teacher in a diverse, urban school;

- Jayne, a middle school English as a Second Language teacher in whose classroom she focuses much attention on language arts and social studies; and
- Johanna, a kindergarten teacher in whose classroom we see many mathematics, science, social studies, and language arts lessons.

Most examples come from Jayne and Johanna, who teach in a highly diverse, urban district with large populations of ELLs. Both teachers are also authors of this book.

A Note for Readers

In this chapter, we have used some acronyms that you may be unfamiliar with or may find confusing as you read other materials in the field of English teaching and learning. These include **ESL** (English as a second language), **EFL** (English as a foreign language), **TESL** (teaching English as a second language), **TESOL** (Teachers of English to Speakers of Other Languages), **ESP** (English for special purposes or English for specific purposes), and **EAP** (English for academic purposes). In some texts, a similar term, **LEP** (Limited English Proficiency) or simply **language minority**, is used. Among them, ESL, TESL, and ELL are the most commonly used terms within the current U.S. education system. For ease, we refer to the students in our schools whose first language is not English as **English language learners**.

2

Six Principles for Teaching English Language Learners

The Instructional Model

What is currently known about the most effective strategies for teaching diverse populations? In recent decades, many researchers have studied patterns of teaching practice that correlate with high achievement for such populations. These studies have made important advances in understanding instructional approaches for African American students, Appalachian students, and the many immigrant students who are still learning English. These studies and the model of instruction presented in this book are based on a Vygotskian (Vygotsky, 1978) teaching-learning framework that takes into consideration students' culture, history, language, and learning patterns. We will discuss the approach in the language used by the Center for Research on Education, Diversity, and Excellence (CREDE), a center formerly known as the National Center for Research on Diversity and Second Language Learning.

Through multiple studies and reviews of studies, researchers at CREDE found that good teaching of diverse populations, including

English language learners (ELLs), reflects what many know as culturally responsive instruction (Foster & Peele, 2001; Gay, 2002; Ladson-Billings, 1994; Nieto, 1999). Culturally responsive instruction is characterized by careful attention to the linguistic and experiential backgrounds of students in order to explicitly connect instruction to those backgrounds, with a simultaneous intention to keep the curriculum rigorous and expectations for student achievement high.

In a synthesis of studies of what works with diverse populations, Tharp & Dalton (2007) have outlined characteristics of instruction aligned with the concepts and practices of culturally responsive instruction. To start, good teaching involves teachers who know deeply the content they are to teach, who attend to standards and guidelines for teaching content, and who are adaptable to changes in content and technology. Good teaching involves the use of up-to-date materials and is accomplished with support from the school's administration and other teachers in the school. Good teaching involves passion, dedication, interest in, and deep care for students. Good teachers have humor and flexibility.

None of these characteristics is surprising, and they are often those that drive teachers toward education in the first place. But what the research also illustrates is that excellent teaching for diverse populations involves attention to *pedagogy*, a kind of pedagogy that is different from traditional teaching, which has served middle-class White populations for centuries. Pedagogy can be defined as the art and science of teaching and is referred to as the *specific actions* teachers take to accomplish learning in their classrooms (Dalton, 2007). It is the *pedagogy* that has changed in U.S. classrooms in response to more diverse populations. No longer will whole-class instruction, students-in-rows, teacher lectures with students' hands raised for participation, and the like serve the populations of students we have in today's U.S. classrooms. Indeed, instruction that has been successful for diverse populations, especially with ELLs, looks quite different from traditional teaching. CREDE has described this instructional model in five standards. These five standards form the basis of the model we illustrate in this book.

The CREDE Five Pedagogy Standards

The Center for Research on Education, Diversity, and Excellence (CREDE) synthesized an extensive body of research on teaching diverse learners into five standards for effective pedagogy:

1. *Joint Productive Activity* (teachers and students work together on joint products)
2. *Language Learning* across the curriculum (teachers help students apply literacy strategies and language competence in all areas of the curriculum)
3. *Contextualization* (teachers connect instruction to students' experiences)
4. *Rigorous Curriculum* (teachers design instruction to advance understanding at complex levels)
5. *Instructional Conversation* (teachers provide instruction in small groups using academic dialogue as a tool for learning)

Each chapter of this book focuses specifically on one of these standards, although all five standards are illustrated in many of the lesson examples we provide. We provide "indicators" of each standard, examples of each from real classrooms, and tips for making them work in all kinds of classrooms, including elementary, middle, and high mainstream classrooms and one middle school self-contained ESL classroom. Most lessons include more than one standard and sometimes, ideally, all of the standards are illustrated in one lesson. In a few cases, we illustrate where the teacher fell short of full implementation of the standard. In the example that follows in this chapter, we observe how one teacher, Cori, uses the five standards to support students' understanding.

The Model Enacted in Seventh Grade

Cori is teaching her first-period, seventh-grade social studies class of 25 students in a highly diverse middle school. Only 6 students are White, and 12 are ELLs, most of whom are Spanish speakers, but some of whom are also Bosnian, Russian, and German speakers. They have been studying ancient civilizations. On the chalkboard, Cori has listed:

Table 2.1   Objectives for Cori's Lesson

Language Objectives	Content Objectives
1. Students will discuss in pairs differences they see in photographs of today and drawings of ancient times. 2. Students will write and summarize Causes and Effects of flooding. 3. Using new vocabulary, students will dialogue about why Sumeria became a civilization.	1. Students will understand how levees work, as well as the causes and effects of flooding. 2. Students will understand why cities emerge near water, as well as the risks involved. 3. Students will distinguish between ancient water control systems and those of today.

Cori begins the lesson reading aloud these objectives to the students. Then she asks them, "What area of the world did we talk about yesterday? You can check your notes."

"The Fertile Crescent."

"Why do we call it the Fertile Crescent?"

A girl answers in Spanish. Cori, who can speak Spanish (a convenient but not necessary skill for teaching English language learners), responds briefly in Spanish first and then says in English, slowly and deliberately, "Yes, it has a lot of rich soil—it is *fertile*. The land can grow a lot because of all of the water nearby." She asks, "What is another name we use?"

"Mesopotamia."

"Yes, what does this mean?"

"Land between the rivers."

Cori points to the map on the wall. "Would someone come up and show us on the map?" A student comes to the front and shows the area in the Middle East that they are studying.

"Who can remember the names of these rivers?"

Different students answer, "Tigris" and "Euphrates."

Cori asks, deliberately, "What were the people who lived there called?"

"Sumerians."

The review from the previous day continues with a discussion of Sumerian agriculture. The students had read about frequent flooding of rivers and recalled that the Sumerians depended on irrigation systems to control the water around them. After about 15 minutes, Cori leads the students into today's topic. She says, "Maybe if you've been watching the news you will know what this is."

She invites the students to come up to the front of the room and surround her at a table so all can witness a demonstration. Cori has before her a large bowl, with one side of the bowl packed with dirt as if to demonstrate land. From a pitcher, Cori gently pours water into the bowl almost to the level of the "land." Using more dirt, she creates a "levee" on the land side of the bowl, and slowly pours more water. The students witness the water sitting slightly above the land. Cori explains that today's system of controlling water is both similar to and different from what the Sumerians did. She asks, "What would happen if I poke a hole or two in the levee? What will happen if the levee breaks?"

"The water will go to the land," answers one English learner.

"There will be a flood," says another student.

"*Why* might a levee break?" Cori asks.

As the students begin to speculate on this question, Cori holds up one finger to indicate, "Don't speak, think." She has taught them this signal to indicate that some questions require more thinking time than others. After a few seconds, different students offer reasons why a levee might fail.

Cori then asks a student to cut the levee with a tool. He does. The water seeps onto the "land" portion of dirt in the bowl. The students watch, mesmerized.

"See the big mess we have here?" The students nod. Cori then turns on an overhead projector where she has several photographs to show the students. First, she shows them pictures of broken levees after Hurricane Katrina. She asks students to turn to a partner and describe the similarities between the broken levee in the classroom bowl demonstration and what they see on the screen. The students begin to talk, heads turning back and forth from bowl to photographs.

Then, Cori puts up several textbook drawings of what land looked like in ancient Sumeria. She asks the students to turn to their partners and compare what they see in the photos of Sumeria with what they see in the photos of New Orleans's levees. Again, the students talk for a few minutes.

When the group reconvenes, one student explains in Spanish that he saw a video about Katrina and that there are two kinds of levees, those that are broken and those that are about to break. Cori responds to him in Spanish, but then says in English, "Can you say that again, this time in English?"

The student slowly explains in English what he had seen on the video. Cori asks the class, "What does that tell you about levees?" The discussion ensues.

Then, Cori asks the students to go back to their desks for a longer discussion. In this part of the lesson, she asks the students to think about why cities might emerge so close to the water and why people would live next to a levee.

Cori asks the students to get out their textbooks in which they had been reading about Sumeria. She introduces a "Cause-Effect" activity that the students are to do in pairs. Each pair is given a "Cause" of broken levees, and they are to look through their text and recall the newscasts about Katrina as sources for "Effects." After the pairs work together, Cori asks the students to offer responses so she can make a summary of their ideas.

During the process of creating this summary, a lively discussion occurs about the effects of hurricanes today in New Orleans and in the past in Sumeria. They discuss the differences in civilizations, buildings that would have been destroyed, and what gets killed. Cori asks, "What kinds of animals would survive?"

One child raises her hand, but even after a long "wait time," the child cannot respond. Cori says to her, "Would you like to ask someone in your group (with whom she is sitting) to respond?" The child says yes and asks her group in Spanish. Cori and the rest of the class wait. Then, the child says, in English, "Birds."

"Yes, Juana, but why would birds survive?"

"Because they can fly away."

"What other animals can get away?"

Juana pauses, "I think…the ones in the zoo?"

Cori smiles. "Yes, I heard a story on the radio recently about how the animals in the New Orleans zoo survived because the zoo was on a hill."

When Cori revisits the topic about why cities emerge around water, the class gives excellent, historically based reasons why Sumeria emerged as a civilization while other tribes may not have survived. They have a harder time understanding why people live so near the water today. Unfortunately, this discussion has to be delayed until the next time. As the students leave her classroom, it is clear that the students look forward to the next lesson.

Reflection on Cori's Teaching

Below we describe how this lengthy description of one lesson exemplifies the CREDE model of instruction. This elaborate example will help illustrate the standards in ways that provide a window into effective classrooms that serve English language learners.

Cori's lesson above might appear to be simply "good teaching" for all kids. And in one sense, it is. However, because of the specific attention Cori pays to certain teacher behaviors, this lesson is particularly appropriate for ELLs. Why? First, Cori's preparation for her lesson was elaborate and specific for ELLs as well as for the other students in her class. Cori was trained in the Sheltered Instruction Observation Protocol (SIOP) model of instruction (Echevarria et al., 2004), a model of instruction grounded in the CREDE standards. One of the features of the SIOP model is *Preparation*, which provides teachers with ideas on how to prepare lessons when the classroom has ELLs. This SIOP feature, Preparation, includes creating objectives for the lesson that include both the content of what is to be covered in the lesson as well as the language skills that are to be addressed by the lesson. Cori had several objectives in each category, as shown by Table 2.1, and she accomplished each one of them in this lesson.

Unfortunately, because the lesson was so exciting, Cori did not have time to review the objectives at the end of the lesson to be sure students understood what they were to learn; however, this review can take place the following day. The idea is that with an explicit focus on both language and content objectives, the teacher and the students will understand that even within content lessons, language learning is still a focus. These objectives can help keep teachers and students focused so they become metacognitively aware of the learning going on in the lesson as it is happening. Cori's planning was also elaborate in that she brought in materials for a vivid demonstration on how levees work and do not work, which helped her contextualize instruction by connecting what she was teaching about Sumeria to the students' recent experiences.

Cori and the CREDE Standards

This lesson was a good example of the CREDE standards for pedagogy. The five standards of *joint productive activity, language and literacy, contextualization, rigorous curriculum*, and *instructional conversation* are overlapping, interwoven, and work in concert. But in order to make them very clear, we will discuss each standard in light of Cori's lesson.

Joint Productive Activity

The CREDE standard of *Joint Productive Activity* (JPA) means that students work together in small groups to complete a task with the involvement of the teacher at points along the way. JPA often shapes an entire lesson—as the product often drives the process in teaching. In this lesson, students worked in pairs to participate in making a list of "Causes and Effects" of some phenomenon. It is a simple product, and yet, in order for the students to be successful at this product, they needed to see Cori's vivid demonstration and the many photographs and drawings. Teachers can use strategies, graphic organizers, and a variety of other "tools" to organize students for Joint Productive Activity (JPA). Also, to successfully create opportunities for JPA, teachers must also attend to grouping patterns. For example, English language learners should at times work with others who speak their language (when possible), and at other times work with native English speakers. ELLs should work in small groups, large groups, pairs, groups of their choice, and assigned groups. Chapter 3 of this book will provide examples of not only strategies for joint productive work, but also tips for grouping and the day-to-day management of working in small groups with a diverse population of students.

Contextualization

The CREDE standard of *Contextualization* means that teachers connect the lesson with students' past experiences from home, with peers, or previous lessons in school. Cori began with an extensive review of the previous day's lesson, emphasizing key vocabulary such as *fertile*. She linked past and new concepts by comparing ancient Sumeria to vivid current photos of Katrina, a topic on the minds of all Americans at the time. Building background is essential for all learners, but it takes the explicit linking of past to present for ELLs because they are learning content simultaneously with language. Chapter 4 of this book will focus on the many ways teachers can build background or *contextualize* instruction within students' understandings.

Language and Literacy

In the CREDE model, the standard of *Language and Literacy Learning* exemplifies the critical need for ELLs to spend much classroom time speaking, reading, and writing about academic topics. In every subject area, oral language development and literacy learning are as important as the content but also serve as a tool to help students learn the content. Cori provided her students multiple opportunities for oral language learning in just one lesson. Simply, "Turn to a partner and compare...." offers an example of how a teacher can provide multiple opportunities for students to practice academic English in a psychologically safe environment as they first rehearse their responses with peers. This simple strategy provides an efficient way to get many students to participate, rather than simply having one student offer a response to the whole class, which is highly inefficient (although necessary at times). Cori also had her students write in response to the readings they had done and the class lesson on the causes and effects of broken levees. Reading and writing become tools for thinking about and learning the content listed in the objectives. Chapter 5 of this book will provide examples of ways teachers can provide increased opportunities for student academic talk in the classroom. It also will include ways teachers can meaningfully help students engage in reading and writing, even when students struggle with these skills.

Rigorous Curriculum

Cori kept the content of the lesson at a high level, using sophisticated vocabulary and asking high-level questions. Her expectation that students make connections between an ancient civilization and the current news about Hurricane Katrina illustrates her respect for them as learners and her expectation that they be engaged with current events. In this way she maintained a *rigorous curriculum*, another standard of the CREDE model. Further examples of rigorous curriculum and lessons that include complex thinking will be the focus of Chapter 6 and woven throughout the rest of this book.

Instructional Conversation

The final CREDE standard is *Instructional Conversation*, a structured form of dialogue that begins with teachers setting a goal about the content they want students to learn through the dialogic lesson (Goldenberg, 1993; Tharp & Gallimore, 1988). Two research-ers (Saunders & Goldenberg, 1999) who have studied the effects of Instructional Conversations (IC) on English language learners in classrooms define ICs in this way:

> Teacher and students engage in discussion about something that matters to the participants, has a coherent and discern-ible focus, involves a high level of participation, allows teacher and student to explore ideas and thoughts in depth, and ulti-mately helps students arrive at higher levels of understand-ing about topics under discussion (e.g. content, themes, and personal experiences related to a story). (p. 142)

In Cori's lesson, there was only the beginning of an Instructional Conversation. She did many things well. She helped make the les-son matter to her students by bringing in the Katrina story that was on all their minds at the time. She kept the focus of the lesson very clear through the high-level questions she asked. She assisted the students in exploring the connection between an ancient civiliza-tion and the city of New Orleans, bringing her students to higher levels of understanding about both. Yet, unlike Cori's lesson, the ideal instructional conversation occurs in small groups rather than with the whole class to allow for more scaffolding toward new understandings. Chapter 7 will focus in more depth on how to con-duct instructional conversations in diverse classrooms. It will pro-vide tips on questioning, feedback, praise and encouragement, and aspects of equitable participation features such as wait time and turn taking.

Scaffolding the Five Standards

One specific concept we will address in this book is effective *scaf-folding,* which is necessary for highly expert teaching. Scaffolding means providing support of students' understandings at high levels and can occur through joint productive activity or instructional con-versation. For example, scaffolding occurs when the teacher asks probing questions, provides suggestions on a product, provides tools such as graphic organizers for students to complete a task, or models how to work cooperatively in groups. Scaffolding can occur during language learning instruction, such as when teachers pro-vide oral language stems or sentence starters, or during literacy learning, when teachers provide models of expert writing from which students can copy work (see Chapter 3 for an example of expert scaffolding of writing). Scaffolding is accomplished through the use of "tools" (Vygotsky, 1978), of which language is one. The teacher prompts, questions, responds, repeats, elaborates, and adds to students' contributions during academic talk or written work. Teachers provide written tools such as Venn diagrams, or other visual texts to support students. Examples of how teachers scaffold instruction to assist students during instruction will be highlighted in each of the chapters throughout the book.

Another way of referring to the scaffolding teachers provide for English language learners is called *comprehensible input* (Echevarria et al., 2004; Krashen, 1981), which is defined as the means for making content more understandable to English language learners. Teachers attend to pace, repetition of key vocabulary and directions, explicit instruction, clear enunciation, gestures, body language, visual aids, eye contact, and more in order to enable students to remain engaged in classroom activities and discussions, even when they might not understand 100% of what the teacher says. In Cori's lesson, she was careful to be deliberate in her speech. She spoke slowly and enunciated words, repeating vocabulary for emphasis. She used eye contact, gestures, and smiles to keep engagement high. Other examples of how teachers assist in this way will be presented in this book because it is a key feature of good teaching for English language learners.

The following table summarizes how Cori's seventh-grade social studies lesson illustrates the CREDE standards for effective pedagogy for ELLs. In addition, we add other notable features of Cori's instruction, including the scaffolding that seems particularly appropriate for her classroom of diverse learners.

Table 2.2   CREDE Standards in Cori's Classroom

Cori's Activity	CREDE Pedagogy Standard	Other Important Features
Created content and language objectives		Preparation—Cori has carefully planned content and language objectives
Review of previous lesson (e.g., "Who can remember the names of these rivers?")	Contextualization (connecting to past experiences)	

(Continued)

Table 2.2   (Continued)

Cori's Activity	CREDE Pedagogy Standard	Other Important Features
Encouragement of first language use (e.g., some students used Spanish for clarification)	Language Learning	
Introduction of new vocabulary (e.g.,"fertile")	Language Learning	
Demonstration of levee breaking	Contextualization (connecting to past experiences) (modified) Joint Productive Activity	
Discussion and questioning during demonstration (e.g.,"*Why might the levee break?*" "*What kinds of animals would survive?*")	Language Learning Rigorous Curriculum (instruction to advance to complex thinking) Instructional Conversation (beginning level)	Cori's deliberate but natural pace of language and repetition of questions help English learners understand difficult concepts
Students (orally, in pairs) compare broken levee as demonstrated in classroom with Hurricane Katrina photographs	Rigorous Curriculum Language Learning Contextualization	
Students (orally, in pairs) compare Katrina photos to textbook drawings of ancient Sumeria	Rigorous Curriculum Language Learning	
Students discuss reasons for emergence of cities near water and implications of living near water	Rigorous Curriculum Language Learning	
Cause-Effect Activity Sheet	Joint Productive Activity Rigorous Curriculum Language Learning	Use of"tools"such as reading and writing strategies and visual graphic organizers can be the extra assistance English learners need to make sense of instruction

This Seems Overwhelming. Can I Do It?

Yes, most teachers can, and they can learn to do it well. Teaching through the five standards has a growing body of research on its effectiveness for student learning (Tharp & Dalton, 2007), so the importance of learning how to teach in this way is clear. However, tackling these standards means that teachers need to have a few things in place. They need a belief in the underlying theory about teaching reflected by the standards, a vision of what the standards mean for practice, some time for making changes, and some more time for reflection on what's working and what needs more work and maybe support. The teachers in our professional development and research project have discussed with us their ease and challenge with the standards and, as a result, we have a few suggestions for getting started.

While all the standards work in concert, we suggest that you begin by focusing on including joint productive activity and contextualization into some lessons that you already teach. For example, if you teach about the water cycle in a traditional way, you can contextualize the lesson by building on what students already know, perhaps by eliciting students' understandings and experiences with different forms of water in different weather. To do joint productive activity, you can provide opportunities for pairs or small groups of students to illustrate the water cycle in a variety of ways, with your input into the product. You can reflect on the implementation of these standards using the short guides at the end of each chapter. When you are ready, you can turn your attention to the other standards.

You can build language development into any lesson. Students should have many opportunities to try out their new academic language in all content areas and in every activity. Simply asking students to turn to a partner and explain what they already know about the water cycle is an opportunity for students to practice in a safe way. Then, you can build reading and writing into your lessons, providing varied types of texts for reading and guiding students to write for the purpose of understanding.

Maintaining a rigorous curriculum is not easy, but it is essential. If the water cycle is part of the core curriculum of your district for the grade level you teach, then that is what ELLs of that grade level should be learning about. You can raise the level of rigor through questioning, the joint productive activity, and reading and writing. One of us once observed a high school newcomer class learning about the parts of the plant. While it was clear that some students did not know the English words for "stem" and "root," it was also clear that these students knew plants well. It was an unnecessary lesson for them. ELLs should be exposed to as much of the standard curriculum as possible.

Finally, if teaching about the water cycle, you can invite small group instructional conversation about a text you've read together on the water cycle, asking high-level questions and encouraging thinking. This standard is often the one cited as most difficult to achieve. One reason is the need for a classroom structure within which the teacher and students have established routines and practices so that small-group work is possible. This then enables the teacher to have an instructional conversation with one group while the rest of the class engages in other meaningful small-group or independent work. Another reason for the difficulty, though, is the need for teachers to "give up" some of their "teacher talk." One indicator of good instructional conversations (see Chapter 7) is that teachers speak less than students, and surprisingly, this is much harder to achieve than to say. Some teachers with whom we have worked have had to watch themselves on video to see that they were doing virtually all the talking, and therefore the thinking. Yet, there is a growing body of research on how teachers develop these skills and the powerful impact they have on student learning (Billings & Fitzgerald, 2002; McIntyre, Kyle, & Moore, 2006).

The remainder of this book is devoted to helping teachers ease into the kind of teaching described by the model above. Each chapter provides illustrations of how several classroom teachers have made efforts to illustrate the five standards in their own practices. We can learn a great deal from them and turn first to the discussion of joint productive activities in teaching.

3

Joint Productive Activity (JPA) and English Language Learners

Seventh-grade language arts teacher Vickie stands next to an overhead projector in front of the class. The class has been working on learning to write memoirs, to "put the writer in the writing" and to describe "a moment." Vickie explains to the students that they will be "looking for evidence from your writing that shows that this 'moment' was special for you." Vickie then shares examples of students' memoirs from her class of the past year that exhibit the kind of evidence she is expecting in their drafts. About one example, she asks, "Do you know the purpose of the piece?"

The students agree that yes, the purpose is clear.

Vickie asks, "What is it?"

A student responds, and Vickie answers, "Yes, a moment when she [the character] realizes she is loved." After more examples, Vickie tells the students to take out the memoirs they have been working on and asks them to look at their texts to see if they have moments that might illustrate a new insight.

One student offers, "Like...that was the moment I realized he depended on me...."

Another student shares how she realized how much she loves her grandfather and how sad she would be if he died.

Vickie nods and says, "Sometimes you don't realize what you've got until it is gone."

Another student looks at his papers and says, "I realized I would always have someone who looks up to me."

Another student says, "Mine is about if you're not feeling good, like you aren't perfect, it's okay to make mistakes."

This lesson sequence continues with more analysis of students' texts for other features of good writing, such as sensory details and dialogue that help readers recall information. Then, Vickie distributes a worksheet to small groups of students (2–3 to a group) that has space for summarizing what was stated and accompanying space for what the statements show. The groups are purposefully designed to have students who are still learning English work with more language-proficient peers. Vickie explains that the students are to read the text together and indicate on the worksheet examples in which the author (Vickie herself) *shows* something to readers rather than *tells*. The students begin their work. One girl murmurs to another, "I can just imagine her [Vickie as a young girl] riding that horse with her skinny legs holding on tight!" Her partner, an immigrant from Bosnia, agrees, "Oh, I know! It's so detailed!"

After several minutes, Vickie gets the students' attention and asks for examples in which she *shows* (in her writing) but does not tell readers what to see or think. She says, "Many of you are quoting places where I *tell* and not show, and those are not the places with the better writing. I want scenes where I actually *prove* how Fury [the horse in the story] gave me freedom."

Show or Tell?

On the left side of the first box below, copy the text (or a portion of it) from the reading that *tells* the reader something (e.g., a description of something, or an action), Then, on the right side of the box, write what you think it shows.

In the second box, find three examples of text in which the author *shows* you something without telling you.

Table 3.1   Vickie's Graphic Organizer for Descriptive Writing

Tell	*Show*
She turned around and walked quickly away.	She was angry.
Showing	

Reflection on Vickie's Teaching

This teaching example is an illustration of several CREDE standards of pedagogy in action. Vickie's lesson *contextualizes* instruction by connecting to previous learning experiences as well as personal experiences. It is focused on *language learning,* specifically writing. It is highly *rigorous* in that she accepts nothing less than a fine-grained analysis of the text. The highlighting feature of her teaching in this lesson, though, is her *joint productive activity*. Having students work jointly on analyzing text using a graphic organizer as a tool is a typical example of Joint Productive Activity, or JPA. This chapter will focus on the specific indicators of JPA and the many ways teachers can design lessons around JPA for maximum learning by all students. Before we provide these examples, we begin with a rationale and a detailed definition of Joint Productive Activity.

Rationale and Definition of JPA

Teachers often have students work together to learn. In many elementary classrooms, for example, teachers who use a "workshop" approach to literacy or mathematics instruction rely on group work that enables students to assist one another while the teacher works with a particular group. Classrooms that operate with this approach are based in sociocultural theory. The key perspective of this theory is the view that teaching and learning are social, not individual, activities. Learning takes place when novices and experts work together to solve a common problem or produce a common product (Rogoff, 1990; Tharp & Gallimore, 1988). A sociocultural model for teaching and learning therefore involves "assisted performance" (Tharp & Gallimore, 1988), in which a teacher or peer helps a student accomplish something he or she may not be able to do alone. Vickie provides opportunities for students who do not yet have language sophisticated enough to analyze text to work with more proficient writers, one of whom is Vickie herself. In joint productive activity, the roles of student and teacher are more permeable and flexible than in traditional models of instruction in which the teacher is always the expert and deliverer of information and the student is always the passive receiver of information.

Joint Productive Activity (JPA) is the use of a particular activity that is collaborative, requires a joint product, and involves the teacher or other experts. Students can often serve as peer experts while the teacher is working with another group. Certainly, the instructional setting in which JPA takes place will look quite different from traditional teaching.

Is This JPA? Indicators of Joint Productive Activity

CREDE has outlined a number of "indicators" of each of the five pedagogy standards. These indicators are like benchmarks (Dalton, 2007) that can be used to assist teachers toward full implementation of the standard. For full implementation of JPA, the teacher proceeds as indicated below.

Indicators of JPA

The teacher
- designs instructional activities requiring student collaboration to accomplish a joint product.
- matches the demands of the joint productive activity to the time available for accomplishing them.
- arranges classroom seating to accommodate students' individual and group needs to communicate and work jointly.
- participates with students in joint productive activity.
- organizes students in a variety of groupings, such as by friendship, mixed academic ability, language, project, or interests, to promote interaction.

> ## Indicators of JPA *(continued)*
>
> - plans with students how to work in groups and move from one activity to another, such as from large-group introduction to small-group activity, for cleanup, dismissal, and the like.
> - manages student and teacher access to materials and technology to facilitate joint productive activity.
> - monitors and supports student collaboration in positive ways.

Vickie's lesson exemplified most of the above indicators. The pairs of students, matched so they can assist each other, spent their time in meaningful analysis of the written text and created products that outlined the differences in an author's text when she "shows" readers her story as compared to when she "tells" them her story. The task was easily accomplished during the one class period, students sat at tables alongside their partners, and Vickie monitored the work by going from pair to pair, assisting as needed.

At the end of this chapter, as with all chapters on the CREDE standards, we provide another way for teachers to examine their own teaching to answer the question, "How do I know if I am doing—?" We recognize that, possibly, the language used to describe the standards may seem familiar, and teachers may wrongly associate them with other instructional practices. Or, the language may seem foreign, and teachers may not realize they already practice many of the indicators of each of the standards. The guides at the end of each chapter may help teachers clarify how well their own practice has developed with respect to these instructional standards.

Classroom Culture

In order for teachers to successfully implement joint productive activity, the classroom culture and climate must be one of respect and high expectations. Teachers must like and care about all of the students and let them know it. Teachers must hold high expectations, communicating always that the students can do the task and work cooperatively together. In return for the respect teachers show students, the students agree to participate in the work with little off-task behavior. Indeed, in contrast to classrooms focused on the CREDE standards, students in traditional classrooms have little choice in student work or in decision making, and consequently, attempts at group work are met with chaos, resistance, or disengagement (Finn, 1999; McIntyre et al., 2006).

A democratic-style classroom that implements the CREDE standards puts the teacher in a complex, delicate position—instead of lesson controller, the teacher becomes lesson facilitator. The classroom is characterized by a problem-solving environment, student decision making, student choice, and much opportunity for student talk about the academic topics. However, in these classrooms, the negotiating may not always be peaceful and easy. When children are asked to negotiate decisions, not all get their wish every time (Lensmire, & Cazden, 1994; Lewis, 1997), but when disruptions do occur, important lessons can be learned, and they set the stage for additional learning.

Of course, a democratic classroom culture is not one in which students make all the decisions and choose all their work. Rather, it is one that reflects guidance from the teacher, intervention when necessary, and a constant nudging toward high-level work (McIntyre et al., 2006). The classrooms described in this book are all characterized by this sort of democratic philosophy in which the teachers care for and respect the students.

For instance, in Jayne's classroom, the students sit at round tables, which allows them to socialize with one another. Middle school students are very social and love to talk (what student doesn't?), and the round table setup allows them to chat with one another as they are working on projects. This setup also requires them to monitor their own behavior because it is easy to get distracted talking with friends and forget what the task is. Also, Jayne tries to allow students to choose their own seats so that they can sit with their friends, with the caveat that if they agree they are getting too distracted to work, they will have to change seats.

When the students work in small groups, Jayne also encourages them to choose partners, or groups. There is a reading corner, with pillows and a rug. Because sitting in the corner is very popular, and Jayne wants everyone to have a turn sitting there, she has "tickets" created and distributed to the students. During independent reading, any four students can each give Jayne one of their tickets to the reading corner. Each student gets four tickets, which they put their name on, and once all the students have used up all their tickets, Jayne simply reissues them. This has worked well; before this system, students squabbled about whose turn it was, and Jayne was arbitrary in choosing the students. Now, it is more equitable, as they get to choose when they want to use their tickets; once four students have given Jayne a ticket, the students know the reading corner is full.

It is important to balance a sense of democracy and student choice with a clearly defined daily structure and routine. Structure and routine allow students to feel that the classroom is a safe place—one where they have some control over their day because they know what to expect when they enter the classroom each day. They don't have to be told what to do over and over again when they walk in the door, such as when to do group work or when to do independent reading. So, the framework giving the day structure is there, but Jayne also tries to vary how she delivers a particular lesson and the kinds of activities the class does together, to keep students interested and engaged in what they are learning together. Jayne knows that the more interactive the instruction, the more the students will be engaged, and the more the students and teacher can build a sense of community. Lately, Jayne increasingly finds herself taking time with a lesson or topic, really trying to listen to students and getting them to listen to one another. The relationships that she builds with students—and that the students build with one another—help build a positive classroom environment where deep and rich learning can take place.

In Johanna's school, the teachers and students follow a management program called CHAMPs, which is based in part on the philosophy that if students know what is expected of them, many problems can be avoided (Sprick, Garrison, & Howard, 1998). Each time there is a transitional period in Johanna's room, the students gather at the carpet and review the CHAMPs expectations:

C—What is the *correct* voice level students can use?
H—What do students do if they need *help*?
A—What *activity* will the students be doing?
M—What type of *movement* is appropriate?
P—How will all of us *participate* together?

A schedule of the day is posted on the wall with illustrations for each period. Students who cannot read or speak English can look at the pictures to know what is coming next. The day begins with the students eating breakfast in the cafeteria and ends with the students getting on the bus to go home. One student has the job of moving an arrow down to the next period as the day progresses so students have a visual aid to help them understand exactly what to expect. Each time there is a transition, the class not only reviews the expectations but also sings transitional songs. For example, the students sing a specific song for cleaning up, lining up, sitting at the carpet, and so on.

The students share the responsibility of creating a "classroom community." Each time a visitor enters the classroom, the entire class says together, "Welcome to our classroom," and continues with the activity. Many of the students hold important jobs that teach values, such as "hugger," "official welcomer," and "caretaker." The hugger is the person who is in charge of giving people hugs when they need or want them. The official welcomer counts to three to remind students to greet any visitors who enter the classroom. Anytime someone gets hurt in the classroom or on the playground, the caretaker makes sure the student is okay.

Throughout the day, the students complete most of their activities in small groups such as reading, math, and science groups. This gives the students an excellent opportunity to learn how to work in small groups. It also gives Johanna's ELL students ample time to practice speaking in both instructional and conversational English.

The students get many opportunities to make choices throughout the day. Students get to pick what learning center they would like to go to. Once they have finished their work in small groups, they have the option of reading a book or completing extra work in the "to do" bucket.

Lastly, Johanna's class has many opportunities to make decisions as a class. The class often votes between two books for story time or decides what songs they would like to sing during singing time. If the students are having difficulty with something in the day, the class discusses what they could do to solve the problem. The class also takes turns writing letters to each one of the students' families. The families often write back to the class, and the students enjoy reading their letters.

The Juggling Act: Grouping and Scheduling of JPA

To create a classroom climate of respect and joint decision making, teachers must have a repertoire of skills for helping students to get and stay engaged in challenging work. One of those skills is learning how to group students in a variety of ways. Most successful JPA occurs in small groups so that participation by all students is ensured. For some activities, the best kind of grouping is in pairs; for other activities, five persons might be the best grouping. When groups are larger than five, there is usually a risk that one or more students can avoid participating without much notice. Many times, teacher will plan the groups, but all groups do the same task. At other times, the teachers plan different tasks for different groups to differentiate instruction based on the needs of students.

In some classrooms that concentrate pedagogy on the CREDE five standards, students participate in joint productive activity in ways commonly known as "centers." That is, students will work together on some activity previously planned by the teacher that is carefully aligned with the goals of the lesson or unit of study. The challenge for the teacher is to design activities that can be completed by students without the teacher while simultaneously challenging them. You will read an example of how this can happen in a middle- or high-school classroom later in this chapter.

Whether the teacher groups students to work on the same task (as shown earlier in Vickie's class) or creates "centers" with varying tasks (as in Justin's class described below), it is important to vary the group roster across a week or month so that students work at times with those who are most similar to them regarding language and/or developmental levels. At other times, teachers should create heterogeneous groups so that students with differing strengths can offer their skills toward the joint product. Of course, at times the teachers should allow students to choose their own groups based on friendships or the tasks they want to engage in. The idea is that students will learn from one another when they are engaged in meaningful activity—what and how much they learn might be determined by the makeup of the group. Thus, groups should periodically be changed.

We have one important caveat about group work. There are many kinds of group work that happen in the classroom. Sometimes it might include students who are doing independent work, such as during the writing workshop, but who ask questions and help one another with the process of writing along the way. This is an example of a low-level sort of JPA, not full JPA that reaps the rewards of new learning. True JPA means that students work *together* on a product. This changes the work immediately because students have to focus on the end product, which shapes the process of the work. True JPA also means the joint product is developed with some assistance by the teacher. Of course, this means teachers cannot usually implement

JPA fully at all times, but must decide when and whom to assist. The example below has students involved in various sorts of JPA. At times, students work together to produce a joint product, and in some cases, the teacher, Justin, also scaffolds the product of the students, illustrating all the indicators of full JPA.

Example of JPA in a Study of Race and Racism

The following example comes from a high-school classroom in which the teacher, Justin, integrated science, social studies, and literature for a study of race and racism. The class was scheduled for 90 minutes of "block scheduling," and the students were reading the novel *Fallen Angels* (Myers, 1989), a coming-of-age story about racism among American soldiers during the Vietnam War, as part of the overall unit. Justin borrowed much of his lesson from the American Anthropological Association's Web site on race (http://www.understandingrace.org), which provides much information about race and racism, as well as instructional units and resources for teachers. He implemented much of the suggested unit using the CREDE five standards for pedagogy. To do so, he used what Dalton (2007) calls "the instructional frame," which includes (1) Briefing, (2) Activities, and (3) Debriefing. Teachers begin each unit or lesson sequence with a "briefing" or "introduction" that gives an overview of the lesson or unit and in which some major concepts may be directly taught. This is followed by the simultaneous activities in small groups, which is the "center" approach that Dalton (2007) calls "multi-tasking." The "activities" are the opportunities for joint productive activity (JPA). The frame ends with a "debriefing," or a review of what was learned, and often a performance to showcase the learning. This frame can be accomplished in one lesson or it can be stretched to a week or more. In Justin's unit on race, his "frame" lasts for one week and most of the activities include some sort of JPA.

On Monday, Justin's "briefing" began with an introduction of the topic of genetic variation and the concept that certain traits, including race, vary along a continuum and that dividing the continuum is arbitrary. His goal was to help students begin to contemplate race not as a biological construct, but more as historically, socially, and culturally constructed. He began by asking his students, "Who thinks of yourself as short?" and "Who thinks of yourself as tall?" After a bit of argument about who is short and tall, he lined up his students by height. He asked where in the continuum of height the students would divide themselves into two groups of "short people" and "tall people." More arguments ensued, and students argued for other categories, such as "average." But even adding a category did not make all students comfortable in which group they "ended up." Justin explained it was the same with race when we see race as only a biological idea. He explained that height and race are "continuous" traits and compared them to discrete traits such as sex, handedness, or blood type. He then showed pictures of many people of all types of skin color and had the students participate in the same analysis and discussion about skin color. The students worked in groups of three to rank and categorize the photos, their first JPA for this unit. If Justin had had a more diverse group of students with respect to skin color, he would have done the "lining up" activity with skin color as well. Instead, he used pictures. Of course, teaching a unit on race and racism requires trusting relationships between students and teacher, something Justin works hard on all year. We write more about the development of community in classrooms later in this chapter.

At the end of the class on Monday, Justin explained to the students that on Tuesday and Wednesday they would participate in "centers" in small groups, and that for some activities they would be expected to produce a joint product. Justin explained he would lead Instructional Conversations about the novel as one of the center activities. He had planned six different activities he believed would help the students come to new understandings about race. As stated, many of the ideas from his lessons came directly from the Web site of the American Anthropological Association's site on race and racism.

On Tuesday and Wednesday, the students worked in groups of four or five and participated in three different centers with their groups, each for 30 minutes. The following day, the six groups participated in the centers they had not yet been to. This kind of teaching is familiar to some elementary teachers who use a workshop approach for reading instruction, and the organization and scheduling is similar. The first "center" was an Instructional Conversation with Justin about the novel. The others included

- Center 2: Exploring world skin color distribution and frequency on the Internet;
- Center 3: Exploring cultural variation (taking a cultural IQ test) from the AAA site;

- Center 4: Exploring dialect (taking a regional dialect quiz and examining patterns of Appalachian and Black English Vernacular);
- Center 5: Exploring the AAA Web site's quiz on race and sports and athletic ability; and
- Center 6: Watching a movie of *The Story of Race* and beginning to write a skit in response to the movie.

Justin's scheduling looked like this: On Wednesday, Justin and the students "debriefed" about each of the centers. Justin had the students think, talk, read, and write about what they had learned. They reflected on big ideas concerning the arbitrariness of categories of race and reasons why we seem to need to categorize. They held discussions on some people's apparent hatred toward people of color and why this might be. He corrected misunderstandings that arose and helped students make connections from their exploratory work on race and the novel they were reading. At the end of the class period, Justin prepared the students for their final group assignments for the next day by explaining their options for a group performance, which included the following:

1. Develop their skits in response to the film more fully for performance before another small group or the whole class;

2. Create a visual display (poster, collage, mural) in response to one of the joint activities that week;

3. Produce an essay or other narrative in response to the unit;

4. Create a research tool (e.g., student survey) to find out more about race and race relations in the school.

The students were given explicit guidance on how to begin each task and were assisted with making choices about which task to choose and with whom to work. They were provided all materials. They were also given a rubric for how the work would be evaluated. One criterion was that the product must illustrate an understanding of the primary concepts taught that week. On Friday, the students began to work on their group performance products to be shared with the class the following week.

Table 3.1   Tuesday's Schedule in Justin's Classroom

	9:00-9:30	9:30-10:00	10:00-10:30
Group A	Center 1: Instructional Conversation about the readings (with Justin)	Center 2: Exploring world skin color distribution and frequency on Internet	Center 3: Exploring cultural variation (taking a cultural IQ test)
Group B	Center 4: Exploring dialect (taking a regional dialect quiz)	Center 5: Exploring AAA Web site on race (quiz on race and sports and athletic ability)	Center 6: Watching movie *The Story of Race*; writing skit in response to movie
Group C	Center 6: Watching movie *The Story of Race*; writing skit in response to movie	Center 1: Instructional Conversation about the readings (with Justin)	Center 2: Exploring world skin color distribution and frequency on Internet
Group D	Center 3: Exploring cultural variation (taking a cultural IQ test)	Center 4: Exploring dialect (taking a regional dialect quiz)	Center 5: Exploring AAA Web site on race (quiz on race and sports and athletic ability)
Group E	Center 5: Exploring AAA Web site on race (quiz on race and sports and athletic ability)	Center 6: Watching movie *The Story of Race*; writing skit in response to movie	Center 1: Instructional Conversation about the readings (with Justin)
Group F	Center 2: Exploring world skin color distribution and frequency on Internet	Center 3: Exploring cultural variation (taking a cultural IQ test)	Center 4: Exploring dialect (taking a regional dialect quiz)

Reflection on Justin's Teaching

In Justin's short unit on race, he exhibited all the CREDE standards for pedagogy. He *contextualized* the new concepts to be learned in students' prior experiences and understandings about personal traits when he asked them to line up and discuss height as a trait. He provided opportunity for much student *language and literacy development* through the centers in which students participated in academic talk and reading and writing a variety of texts. The *curriculum was rigorous,* with much thinking about important, complex ideas, and he conducted small-group *Instructional Conversations* about the novel. Of course, the many small-group activities in the centers were examples of JPA, as were the students' final performance activities.

JPA in Middle School ESL:
Learning From Our Mistakes

Testing is a normal part of schooling, one that typically neither students nor teachers care much for. Yet, it is also a necessity and one that can be productive, fun, and a real opportunity for both language and content learning. Because students are always anxious to find out how well they did on tests, this joint productive activity should be conducted prior to returning the tests, since this is a time when you will most likely have their undivided attention!

Jayne assigns each student a partner—someone that student feels comfortable with—because this activity involves lots of conversation. Two students who don't know each other very well might have a hard time getting started and staying focused on this type of activity. Jayne has the students begin by reading aloud to each other, one by one, each question that either of them missed on the test. The students read the entire question, including all the possible answers. Jayne explains that the purpose of this activity is *not* just to find out the correct answer to each test question, but to discover *why* they chose the answer they did, to be metacognitive and think about and discuss their own thought processes in choosing their answers.

After the question is read aloud, students who selected the correct answer should explain to their partner why they chose the answer they did, indicating both *why* and *how* they eliminated the wrong answers to choose the correct answer. Was it because they remembered studying this particular point? What did they study that helped them with this answer? Or was it because, even though they weren't absolutely sure of the correct answer, they were able to use a process of elimination to choose the answer that made the most sense? This conversation is the heart of this activity, so Jayne makes sure that students understand the importance of metacognitive thinking. If both partners had gotten the answer incorrect, the partners must work together to figure out the correct answer, in either their textbook or their notes. Again, they should be discussing why they got the answer wrong. Was it really because they didn't know the right answer? Or was it something else? As the students are discussing the test with their partner, Jayne circulates around the room and encourages students who may need some extra help, or she lets them know they are on the right track. Jayne hears clear, focused academic conversation at times, and when she does, she lets the students know that this is exactly what they should be doing. Words of encouragement are so important in situations like this because students often are not sure of themselves at first.

Once the partners have finished discussing their answers with each other, Jayne invites them to write a reflective response about this activity. On a piece of paper, an overhead, or an LCD projector, Jayne gives them a prompt in written form, such as one of the following:

- Now that you and your partner have finished your discussion, reflect on what you have learned.
- Beyond the fact that you may or may not have studied sufficiently for this test, what did you learn from your discussion with your partner about multiple-choice tests in general and your own thought processes specifically?
- What do you think you need to do differently next time? What strategies will you use that you did not use this time?

Jayne gives the English language learners time to reflect in writing, which prepares them for the larger class discussion that follows.

As the final step in this process, Jayne asks the students to share with the whole class what they wrote about in their reflection. As students share, Jayne summarizes their reflections visually in a bulleted list for the entire class on a chart, an overhead, or an LCD projector. She points out what they have learned, not only about the content material but also about strategies that are generalizable to any test-taking situation. Prior to the next test, she will be sure to use this summary chart to review and remind them of what they learned. One of the benefits of this activity is that it gives students the opportunity to discover for themselves, with the help of a peer, what they are doing wrong on tests. Students often discover that it is not that they haven't studied. It's that they aren't reading the question carefully enough, or they misunderstood the question entirely. Another important benefit of this activity is that students are discussing and reviewing the academic content you have been teaching them in an authentic context that is meaningful to them. It is amazing what students discover about themselves through this process.

Reflection on Jayne's Teaching

This strategy can be used to focus and encourage Instructional Conversation between and among students and the teacher in any content area. It provides students the opportunity to review content and use language to learn. Further, it helps English language learners to prepare for standardized tests by focusing on the multiple-choice test format. As we all know, there is a strategy to doing well on multiple-choice tests, but this is often an "academic secret" that students are not told about. This joint activity provides an opportunity for teachers to tear away the veil of secrecy and helps students decipher the mystery of how to do well on multiple-choice tests.

Teaching Tips for JPA

- Give students choice in their work or readings as often as you can.
- Plan multiple activities for small groups of students so you as teacher can work with one of those groups in Instructional Conversation (see Chapter 7), or discussion about concepts.
- Plan the groups ahead of time. Decide to group students at times by proficiency, first language spoken, interest groups, friendships, purposes of the project, and so on. Vary groups periodically so all students work with all others at some time.
- Plan for products that can be accomplished in the time span given.

- Realize that some center activities do not need a formal product; having students write for five minutes about what they learned in the center activity can suffice.
- Make rules for participation in groups explicit.
- Demonstrate first whatever you expect students to do.

Assessing JPA in Your Teaching

Researchers and teachers at the Center for Research on Education, Diversity, and Excellence (CREDE) have developed an assessment tool that allows researchers to document teachers' implementation of these standards. We believe the tool asks the kinds of questions teachers can ask themselves for self-assessment of their implementation. The following questions, taken almost verbatim from the Web site, will help you decide which aspects of JPA you are implementing well and which aspects may still need attention.

1. Do my instructional activities require student collaboration to accomplish a joint product?

2. Do the demands of the joint productive activity match the time available for accomplishing it?

3. Does the seating arrangement in my classroom accommodate students' individual and group needs to communicate and work jointly?

4. Do I participate with students in joint productive activity?

5. Do I organize my students in a variety of groupings, such as by friendship, mixed academic ability, language, project, or interests, to promote interaction?

6. Do I ever plan with my students how to work in groups and move from one activity to another, such as from large-group introduction to small-group activity, for cleanup, dismissal, and the like?

7. Do I manage student and teacher access to materials and technology to facilitate joint productive activity?

8. Do I monitor and support student collaboration in positive ways?

4

Contextualization and English Language Learners

Making Learning Meaningful

Johanna's kindergarten students, a group made up of English language learners and native speakers, sit "crisscross, applesauce" in front of her as she directs their attention to posters listing the CHAMPs rules (as mentioned in Chapter 3) and the content and language objectives of today's lesson ("The students will examine and compare the texture of various objects" and "Students will use adjectives"). Johanna reminds the children that they will continue their study of the properties of objects by focusing specifically on texture. She also helps them know that *adjectives* are *words that describe*.

Johanna places a brown paper bag on her lap and invites students to come up one by one to where she's seated on the rocking chair, smiling and saying in an animated and conspiratorial way, "I'm going to hold up an object. I don't want you to look. Close your eyes." One child, Lili, does so as Johanna takes out a chalkboard eraser. Johanna motions to the rest to stay quiet. "I just want you to *feel* the object. What does it *feel* like?"

Lili responds, "Soft."

Johanna repeats, "It feels soft. Anything else?" (Lili shakes her head no.) "OK, guess what it is."

Lili pauses and then guesses, "An eraser."

"She got it!" (Gives Lili a high-five). "What helped her figure out that this was an eraser?"

"She feeled it!"

"She felt it, that's right. And, she used one of our *property* words. What was that?"

Children chorus, "Soft."

Johanna continues the routine with Juan, who reaches his hand into the bag and says the object feels "rough."

Johanna responds, "It feels rough. Very good. And, what do you think this is? *Feel* the shape of it."

"A pointer."

"What kind of pointer, everyone?"

The children respond in chorus, "Magic pointer!"

Johanna repeats excitedly, "It's our magic pointer!" (Gives Juan a high-five.) "So Juan figured out that this was a pointer by doing what?"

"Feeling it."

Johanna reinforces this response: "That's right, by *feeling* the *texture*."

The lesson continues with Johanna asking, "What do you think it *feels* like? What's the *texture*?" Vanessa identifies a soft toy animal, and Lawrence describes his object as "kind of pointy." Johanna immediately notes, "That's a new word!"

The lesson continues as Johanna and the children review their growing list of texture words. Then, Johanna says, "Now, I want everyone to put on their thinking caps. We're going to use our prior knowledge, *things we already know about*. I want you to think about something at home that you could feel the texture of." The children share such things as "the table—kind of hard and kind of soft" and "Batman cape," which Johanna helps the child describe as soft and smooth. Following this, the children work as partners with familiar objects from the room, such as a shell, sandpaper, card paper, a block, a birthday candle, a rock, and a cork, and together categorize them by texture as rough or smooth. After a whole-group sharing, the children then write (or draw) things they label as rough, smooth, or soft. The science lesson ends with a review of the objectives and some more sharing of texture words the children used in their work.

Reflection on Johanna's Teaching

In this vignette, we see that Johanna makes continual references to the children's prior knowledge from previous lessons and to their experiences with items they know from their classroom. Further, she encourages them to think of items in their homes and to decide what words they would use to describe the item's *texture*, repeating and reminding them that this means *how things feel.* Contextualization means that teachers make connections both with previous lessons and with what students know from their homes and communities. It also means being respectful of children's differing ways of interacting in classrooms.

In addition, we see a little evidence of Johanna's teaching of other CREDE standards. First, Johanna implements aspects of a *rigorous curriculum* (see Chapter 6) through the high expectations she holds for all of her students, accompanied by constant scaffolding to help them reach those expectations. She clearly believes the students can respond to the challenges she provides for them and gives them enthusiastic words and "high-fives" to endorse their efforts.

The children engage in *joint productive activity* (see Chapter 3) as they work in pairs to categorize familiar objects according to texture, and students' development of vocabulary is part of her implementation of the *language and literacy* (Chapter 5) standard. But, the focus of the discussion in this chapter is on the standard of *contextualization* and the ways this is shown in Johanna's and other teachers' classrooms.

Meaning of Contextualization

Think of a time when you learned something new from a very good teacher. What did that teacher do that assisted your learning? Probably, the teacher found a way to make your new learning meaningful by connecting it in some way to what you already knew or had experienced. Perhaps you were learning how to prepare Spanish tapas, or set up your fancy new TV (or Ipod or digital camera), or improve your tennis or golf swing. The teacher no doubt found something for you to "hook" your learning to, even if what you had to learn was difficult and stretched you toward new understandings and skills. In essence, this is what "contextualization" means, and it provides an important scaffold for learners—especially English language learners, as they grapple with a new language and the concepts and abstract ideas in the various content areas.

Those writing about a sociocultural or culturally responsive approach to teaching describe effective ways to engage diverse populations in academic learning. They advocate that teachers build from students' cultural experiences and ways of learning and using language to shape instructional events (August & Erickson, 2006; Delpit, 1995; Foster & Peele, 2001; Gay, 2002; Ladson-Billings, 1994; Moll, 1992; Tharp, Estrada, Dalton, & Yamauchi, 2000). Key to this perspective is an attitude of respect for the knowledge students bring with them to the classroom, an effort to discover what students and their families know, and an ability to make meaningful connections as a part of teaching.

Tharp et al. (2000) summarize three types, or levels, of contextualization from the literature—instructional, curricular, and policy.

- In the opening vignette, Johanna demonstrates contextualization at the instructional level. She connects what needs to be learned to the children's existing schema about objects' properties and texture and to their environment and experience (Tharp & Gallimore, 1988) as they felt, described, and identified familiar items from the classroom.

- Johanna's lesson also demonstrates another kind of contextualization at the curricular level that happens when teachers find a way to incorporate what students know from their home contexts into their learning at school. In this case, the children drew on their "funds of knowledge" (Moll & González, 2004)—that is, the familiar practices and knowledge of households and communities—to identify the textures of things in their homes.

- The third, or policy, level of contextualization involves collaborative work among parents, communities, and schools in shaping educational programs together. While the example does not illustrate this, an increasing number of resources exist and are available to review and learn from. The Center on School, Family, and Community Partnerships at Johns Hopkins University (http://www.csos .jhu.edu/p2000/center.htm), the National Center for Family and Community Connections with Schools (http://www .sedl.org/connections/) associated with the Southwest Educational Development Laboratory (http://www.sedl.org/ welcome.html), and the special-interest group on Family, School, Community Partnerships of the American Educational Research Association (https://www.aera.net/) offer many examples of projects, ongoing research, and related materials.

Two additional points about contextualization are important to consider. First, focusing on the goal of contextualizing learning in ways that build from students' prior knowledge and experiences both in and outside the classroom in no way means that teaching should focus only on what students already know. Just imagine how little any of us would know if this were true! Students need to stretch toward new understandings and to grapple with unfamiliar content. The point is how teachers can help them with that stretching and grappling. Making it all meaningful by grounding it in the known and familiar provides that needed help. The purpose of this chapter is to provide examples of how some teachers are doing that successfully.

Second, at times the teacher must create the known and familiar before moving on instructionally. Given the diversity in today's classrooms, not much commonality exists. So, the teacher must help the classroom community develop shared experiences that then become the basis, in part, for the contextualization of the learning that will take place. As Tharp et al. (2000) note,

> In multicultural classrooms, teachers can create shared experiences through activity-based and problem-oriented instruction, shared activities, and a vigilant seeking of opportunities to invoke and instructionally use students' individual experiences and knowledge, especially in teacher-student dialogue. (p. 29)

Are We Connecting?
Contextualization is Making Meaning

The Center for Research on Education, Diversity, and Excellence (CREDE) identifies eight indicators that illustrate teachers' practices in contextualizing their instruction (http://crede.berkeley.edu/standards/3cont.shtml). These indicators can serve as a helpful checklist of reminders for teachers as they plan curriculum units and daily lessons.

Indicators of Contextualization

The teacher

- begins activities with what students already know from home, community, and school.
- designs instructional activities that are meaningful to students in terms of local community norms and knowledge.
- acquires an awareness of local norms and knowledge by talking to students, parents or family members, and community members, and by reading pertinent documents.
- assists students to connect and apply their learning to home and community.
- plans jointly with students to design community-based learning activities.
- provides opportunities for parents or families to participate in classroom instructional activities.
- varies activities to include students' preferences, from collective and cooperative to individual and competitive.
- varies styles of conversation and participation to include students' cultural preferences, such as co-narration, call-and-response, and choral, among others.

Considering that English language learners face the daunting challenge of not only acquiring a new language but also understanding the nuances of using that language, the ability of the teacher to contextualize ELLs' learning becomes critical. What does this look like in practice? Similar to the opening vignette above, additional examples follow.

Examples of Contextualization

In the following examples, we see how Jayne (in her middle school language arts classroom), Johanna (in another lesson with her kindergarten students), and Linda (in her fourth-grade science and mathematics lessons) each make a lesson's academic content meaningful for their students. Across the examples, varied ways of contextualization become apparent as the teachers make connections to both the students' out-of-school experiences and prior learning within the classroom. Note, for example, how Jayne helps students visualize a scene with familiar food and connects with students' love of music. Johanna, with her kindergarteners, taps into what they know about different fruits as they sequence events in an engaging picture book. And, Linda uses role-playing and common objects from the classroom to convey concepts in science.

Contextualization in Middle School Language Arts

Contextualizing new knowledge could be as simple as asking explicitly for students to make connections to their own experiences in order to understand a larger concept. In a recent lesson on understanding the purpose of text features, Jayne started out her lesson by telling a story to her students.

"Imagine it's a beautiful Saturday afternoon. You and some of your friends are at the park playing soccer. You've been there all day and now everyone is really hungry. One of your friends has a cell phone and so you all pool your money to order an extra large pizza. You can't wait for the pizza to arrive, and when it finally does, you pay the driver and he speeds off into the distance. But when you open up the pizza box, to your complete surprise and dismay, you find that they've forgotten to cut your pizza into slices! All you have is one giant pizza! There's no knife or pizza cutter in sight!"

"How's everyone going to get some pizza when it's not cut up into slices?" says one student.

"Yeah. It's going to be almost impossible to eat it!" says another.

"That's right." says Jayne. "You have to eat the pizza one slice at a time, one bite at a time, don't you? Imagine trying to pick up a whole extra large pizza and eating it! What a mess that would be! Well, it's the same when we try to read a whole long article in a textbook or magazine. If we try to read it all at once, it's almost impossible to digest all of it. That's why writers chunk their informational writing using text features such as text boxes, side-bars, headings, subheadings...."

From there the lesson continues as students open up their magazine article and work at identifying text features and discussing their purpose while working in small groups. This provides an opportunity for *joint productive activity,* as described in Chapter 3. By connecting the idea of chunking information to the story about trying to eat a whole, uncut pizza, students are much more likely to remember both the term *chunking* and the purpose of text features, since they all will understand the importance of cutting up something as large as a pizza into manageable slices. They are also engaging in *language and literacy* activities (see Chapter 5).

Another way to contextualize learning for middle school students is through the use of music and technology. Today's students are "tuned in" to technology and music of all kinds. As part of the content for middle school writing in Jayne's district, students in Language Arts classes were given the daunting task of writing a ballad. One of the first lessons in the unit requires that students read the poem, "The Ballad of Birmingham." While this ballad is a powerful example of the genre, today's students don't always relate to the one-dimensional experience of simply reading a poem out loud. In order to liven up the lesson and connect the experience to the students' own love of music and the World Wide Web, Jayne went online and found archived copies of the original newspaper article upon which the "Ballad" was based, along with photographs of the bombing, and two different versions of the "Ballad of Birmingham" put to music.

Using an LCD projector and a laptop computer, Jayne shared with the students photographs of the bombing, gave them a chance to read some of the original article about the bombing, and then projected the poem onto the screen as they listened to the "Ballad" being sung. The students were able, through the use of music and technology, to understand the ballad genre in a very memorable way. Many of the students wanted to know more about why the bombing occurred, and one student was so intrigued by the story that she did some research on her own and came back to class the next day with a newspaper article about a man who had recently been arrested for the crime. This kind of contextualization provided a way of making sure a *rigorous curriculum* (see Chapter 6) was implemented and also allowed the students to develop a curiosity and interest in the genre ballad that Jayne was able to build upon in subsequent lessons.

Contextualization in Kindergarten

Johanna's students sit "crisscross, applesauce" in front of an easel holding a big book, *The Very Hungry Caterpillar* by Eric Carle. The students go over the objective, which is to recognize the sequence of events. Johanna asks, "Who can tell me what that means?"

Gabby replies, "It means to remember what happens in the story."

"Excellent, Gabby!" Johanna says.

The class then sings the story time song, "Story time is here. Story time is here. I have a story for you. Story time is here. This is the front of the book. This is the back of the book. This is the spine of the book. Yeah!" Johanna points to the correct parts of the book as they sing. She uses songs often as a way to extend the many *language and literacy* (see Chapter 5) experiences in the classroom.

Before the story is read, Johanna asks the students to make a prediction about what will happen in the story. Juan says, "I think the caterpillar is going to eat a whole lot!"

Johanna replies, "What a great prediction, Juan! Has anyone ever eaten a whole lot of food before and gotten a stomachache?" Many of the students raise their hand.

"I have lots of good food here that the caterpillar has already eaten! Would you like to see some of the things he's eaten?" All the students yell out, "Yes!"

"Let's see what the caterpillar sunk his teeth into!" Johanna says excitedly and reaches for puppets that are illustrations of all the food eaten in the story. "Who can tell me what some of these foods are called?" asks Johanna. The children raise their hands eagerly and Vanesa says, "Apple," pointing to the apple puppet.

"Yes! This is called an apple, Vanesa. Good job! Have you ever eaten an apple before?" asks Johanna.

Vanesa smiles and replies, "Yes."

"Then you will be able to make a text-to-self connection with the story, won't you?"

Several more students name some of the food puppets as Johanna hands a piece to each child. As Johanna reads the story, the students hold up their piece of food when it is their turn. Throughout the story, Johanna reminds the students of their objective: to remember the sequence of events in the story. Once the book has been read, the students work together in small groups to put the puppets in the correct order they appeared in the story, a good example of the use of *joint productive activity* (see Chapter 3).

To conclude the story, Johanna creates a T-chart with the heading "One" on the left and "More Than One" on the right. She says, "In our story the caterpillar eats one of some things, and two or more of other things. Can you help me decide which foods go under each column?" One by one, the students take turns writing a type of food on the chart and drawing an illustration to match.

As the lesson concludes, Johanna refers back to the objective. "Boys and girls, did we reach our objective today? Did we sequence the events in the story correctly?" All the students agree that they did. As is evident, the *contextualization* of the story helped the students accomplish the goal of learning how to sequence events. Johanna engaged these kindergarteners in much conversation focused on *literacy and language* (see Chapter 5).

Contextualization in Fourth-Grade Science and Mathematics

About one-third of the 24 students in Linda's fourth-grade class are English language learners whose families have immigrated to the United States from countries such as Mexico, Cuba, Bosnia, and Puerto Rico. Linda begins a science lesson by writing both content and language objectives on the board and having the students, who sit in groups of four, read them with her.

Linda directs them. "Let's read the content objectives. These are what I hope you will understand more about after today's lesson: What makes light, and what are two kinds of light? Be able to name and explain three kinds of objects that light can react to."

Linda then has them review the language objectives. "This is what I want you to understand—when you hear a word, be able to say it, be able to read it, and be able to write it. Use the words *natural, artificial, transparent, translucent,* and *opaque* when talking about light."

After having the students work together in pairs to read the words on word strips and talk together about what they think the words mean, Linda builds from the students' prior knowledge and items they are familiar with in the classroom to help them understand the new and challenging science terms.

Linda walks over to the classroom window to point outside. "This window is *transparent* because I can see what is on the other side. It is *transparent*." She then has one of the students stand up and notes, "When I put my hand behind his back, you cannot see my hand. He is *opaque* because you cannot see through him." She continues by showing *natural* flowers that are "made from nature," and *artificial* flowers made from plastic. Finally, Linda holds up a piece of cloth in front of her face and asks, "Can you see me through the cloth?" The children respond, "A little," and Linda says, "The cloth is *translucent* because you can see through it but what you see is blurry and not clear."

In a subsequent mathematics lesson, Linda continues to contextualize the learning for the students by making connections to their prior learning and experiences both inside and outside of the classroom. For example, in teaching to the content objective—"Know how to change numbers from *standard* to *expanded* to *word* forms"—Linda helped the students who were struggling to understand the expanded form. She reminded them of something familiar: "Think of having a balloon with little tiny writing on it. When you blow it up, you have *expanded* it; you've stretched it out, and you can see the words better. When we write a number in the *expanded* form, we can see each part. So for 20 + 1, we can see that 21 is made up of the value of 20 *plus* the value of 1."

Additionally, in this lesson, Linda contextualizes not only the content but also the cooperative learning process of working as partners. For many of her students who are new to the United States, learning how to "do school" is an important goal. In this instance, Linda must create a shared understanding within the classroom and must build a common background among the students of how to work together.

Linda and her assistants model the process in a "fish bowl" format. The students form a wide circle around the adults in order to observe the demonstration. Linda then notes, "Just as you see fish in a bowl, you can see us learn how to play the game together." After the demonstration, Linda reminds them: "The hardest part of the game is following the cooperative rules. Did we yell at one another? Get up and walk away? Or support one another with suggestions or 'good job' words?"

Reflection on Examples

Laying the groundwork for lessons through contextualization such as those described above sets the stage for teachers to be able to delve deeply into concepts they want their students to learn with the assurance that the new knowledge they are acquiring is simply adding to the students' already well-developed schema, which the teacher has been able to tap into through the contextualization process. Building from the students' prior experiences outside and inside the classroom and creating common understandings become important aspects of teaching.

In the above examples, we see each of the teachers begin with what students know, such as familiar food, classroom objects, and music. Johanna, Jayne, and Linda then build from students' prior understandings and experiences to create meaningful classroom activities related to the intended goals of teaching reading strategies and concepts in science and mathematics. To tap into students' varied learning preferences, the teachers engage the students in both group and individual opportunities to learn. The lessons provide a means for helping the students learn strategies and concepts they can later apply to situations they encounter outside of school as well.

The examples from Jayne's, Johanna's, and Linda's classrooms offer much guidance for other teachers to consider. For example, after taking a careful look at the content you are expected to teach, you might ask yourself questions such as these: How meaningful would this content be for my students? What might they already know about that I could tap into as a "hook"? What could I plan for the class that would develop a shared understanding of this content? How can I build a background of knowledge for all of us to use as we learn more about this topic? What parents or other family members might know something about this topic (or something related to it) that I could try to involve in some way?

Teaching Tips for Contextualizing Instruction

- Ask students to interview parents or other adults at home about interests, talents, and experiences.
- Build into instructional units and lessons ways in which students can share what they know and be expert about a topic.
- Invite parents or other family members to share their expertise related to an instructional topic.
- Examine typical homework assignments to see if they tap into the students' experiences or could be redesigned to do so.

- Find ways during teaching to make incidental connections with students' lives out of school.
- Use Know, Want to Learn, and Learned (KWL) charts and spend time helping students generate ideas about what they already know that has a possible connection to the topic. Students may not realize that their background of experiences relates to school topics until they are helped to see the relationship.
- Provide opportunities for students to relate prior learning in a safe context with partners or small groups before large-group sharing.
- Provide written and visual guides such as graphic organizers to help students contextualize the learning.
- Use many strategies for helping students to learn the needed vocabulary, such as word walls, word sorts, highlighted texts, pictures with words in the classroom, and so on.

Assessing Contextualization of Your Teaching

The questions you may want to ask yourself to assess your implementation of the standard contextualization is also taken from the CREDE Web site. These questions include the following:

1. Do I listen to students talk about familiar topics such as home and community?

2. Do I respond to students' talk and questions, making 'in-flight' changes during conversation that directly relate to students' comments?

3. Do I assist written and oral language development through modeling, eliciting, probing, restating, clarifying, questioning, praising, and so on, in purposeful conversation and writing?

4. Do I interact with students in ways that respect students' preferences for speaking that may be different from the teacher's, such as wait-time, eye contact, turn-taking, or spotlighting?

5. Do I connect student language with literacy and content area knowledge through speaking, listening, reading, and writing activities?

6. Do I encourage students to use content vocabulary to express their understanding?

7. Do I provide frequent opportunities for students to interact with one another and the teacher during instructional activities?

8. Do I encourage students' use of first and second languages in instructional activities?

These indicators overlap and support one another, so it is likely that if you do a few of these, you do all (or nearly all) of them. Implementation of this standard indicates your overall respect for your students, their experiences, and language.

5

Language and Literacy Development for English Language Learners

Consider the following lesson in Johanna's kindergarten classroom of 24 students, including 15 English language learners who speak five different languages. Johanna sits on a low chair next to the carpeted area while her students sit facing her. She holds up a picture book, titled *Who Uses This?* (Miller, 1990). Johanna speaks slowly and distinctly, saying, "The book is titled *Who Uses This?* I am going to read it to you. We are going to look at the illustrations and text features to help store important or new information. Do you know what that means? We are going to look at the pictures to understand the story."

A Mexican American child, a recent immigrant who is still acquiring conversational English, raises her hand. Johanna asks, "What do you see, Claudia?"

Claudia says, "Girl."

Johanna points to the picture of the girl on the book, nods at Claudia, and says to the class, "Good. It is a girl, niña. Good." She tells Claudia, "Point to the boy," and Claudia points to the boy in the book.

Johanna continues. "What else do you see?"

Claudia points to the picture in the book in which someone is using a rolling pin for baking and says, "I did this."

Johanna says, "Ah! A connection!"

Claudia says, "Bowling pin."

Johanna pronounces distinctly, "Rolling pin. Good. Where did you learn this?"

Claudia says, "Mommy."

Johanna says, "Your mommy uses a rolling pin!"

Claudia smiles.

After Johanna begins to read the book, she reaches into a bag next to her chair and pulls out the item pictured in the book. She holds up a hammer and asks, "Who uses this?"

A child says, "A hammer!"

Johanna says, "Yes, a hammer. Touch it and say 'hammer'." Each child does this, murmuring comments about the item to one another.

Johanna continues, "Who uses this? Does anyone that you know build things?"

A child says, "My dad."

A child says, "My mom."

The lesson continues with the reading of the text and interpretation of the pictures. For each new item, Johanna reaches in her bag, pulls out the item, teaches the word orally, points to the word in print in the book, and then has the children say the word and touch the item.

Rationale and Definition of Developing Language and Literacy

This chapter is about CREDE Standard 3, Developing Language and Literacy. Without a doubt, proficiency in speaking, reading, and writing across the curriculum is essential to student and life achievement. This standard is about helping all students improve their speaking, reading, and writing in English and, ideally, in the students' first language as well. In Johanna's lesson, she exemplified many of the indicators of this standard and much more.

Indicators of Language and Literacy Teaching

As with the other standards, the CREDE "indicators" for the Language and Literacy standard provide benchmarks that can be used to assist teachers toward full implementation of the standard. For full implementation, the teacher

- Discusses topics familiar to students, such as home and community, to foster language proficiency in the language of instruction;
- Respects others' preferences for speaking that may be different, including wait time, eye contact, turn taking, spotlighting one student to respond, and use of first language;
- Continuously models vocabulary and syntax and elicits students' verbal expressions;
- Uses phonics and comprehension strategies that ensure all students' literacy at proficient and critical levels; and
- Guides all students to proficient use of spoken and written academic language.

In the short excerpt of her lesson above, Johanna helps students connect their first language and experiences through her choice of the book *Who Uses This?* She models and explicitly points out new vocabulary (e.g., rolling pin) and many other words in the book by actually showing the item and then showing an illustration of it in the book. Johanna assists students in connecting oral vocabulary (e.g., hammer, rolling pin, and many more words) with print reading from the book. Johanna teaches a comprehension strategy of finding meaning through pictures, appropriate for kindergarten age and development. In addition, Johanna elicits students' verbal expressions throughout the lesson, and purposely speaks slowly and distinctly with considerable wait time so that her students understand her. These features of Johanna's instruction and her explicit explanations, close proximity, and eye contact illustrate not only this CREDE standard but also the SIOP principles of *Comprehensible Input* and *Lesson Delivery*.

Johanna's lesson exemplifies more than just the Language and Literacy standard. She also *contextualizes* instruction during the lesson through her use of questioning (e.g., "Where did you learn this?" and "Who uses this? Does anyone that you know build things?"). She also exhibits the CREDE standard of rigorous curriculum. She has high expectations of her kindergarteners. In this short excerpt, she expects these young children to (1) learn new vocabulary, (2) make connections between home experiences and the printed text, and (3) make connections from the actual physical item to the spoken word and to the printed word. She does this through *scaffolded* instruction. For example, she supports Claudia's language development by reinforcing her use of the word "girl" in describing the picture and gently but explicitly correcting with "rolling pin" for Claudia's use of "bowling pin." Showing the picture, saying the name, and touching the object all offer strategies that help expand the children's vocabulary and their understanding of words in context. Finally, Johanna's instruction weaves the goals of the National Reading Panel (National Institute of Child Health and Human Development [NICHD], 2000) with the pedagogy standards of CREDE. This topic will be discussed further later in the chapter.

The Case for Home Language Development

Researchers from such disparate fields as linguistics, psychology, anthropology, and education have shown across decades that people learn concepts through language use. The simple act of talking in meaningful sentences shapes the mind to better use language in the future. It is why therapists have patients talk through issues in order to understand them and why teachers ask students to explain their responses to a piece of literature or talk through the steps of a procedure. It is one of the reasons for the recent push by many literacy educators (Almasi, 1995; Goldenberg, 1993; Many, 2002) for a change in student-teacher discourse so that *students* do the majority of the classroom talking. The same is true for how writing shapes thinking. Both reading and writing assist students in not only learning language but also learning about the topic about which they are reading and writing.

Thus, there is a strong case for promoting the development of oral language and literacy of students' first or home languages (Lesaux, Koda, Siegel, & Shanahan, 2006). Students need to develop their first language in order to develop their minds, and they need to learn to read and write in that first language simultaneously with learning to read and write English. Indeed, the more the students know of their first language, the easier it will be for them to learn subsequent languages, including English.

But how can teachers help students develop in their home language when (1) they do not speak the child's first language, and (2) they are helping the children develop English skills simultaneously? First, the teachers can understand, accept, appreciate, and celebrate the students' home languages. This may mean allowing the children to respond initially to questions or written assignments in their first language and then allowing students to repeat responses in English, as we saw Cori do with her middle school students in Chapter 2. Another simple way teachers can support students' first language is by seating children near others who speak their first language so that students can rehearse responses or "think aloud" (Roehler & Duffy, 1991) in their first language before responding in English. These simple instructional moves illustrate respect for the students' home language and a celebration that these learners will be bi- or multilingual—a true feat for anyone.

Teachers can respect their students' home language by encouraging the families to speak in their native tongues at home. We have heard teachers complain, "My students will never learn English if their parents continue to speak Spanish [or whatever their native language] at home!" Yet, what is critical is that students have good language models. The more the students know about their first language, the better equipped they will be to learn English. Further, families usually speak conversational language at home, not academic language, and many students are already proficient in conversational English. They are not likely to hear academic English at home; thus, a preferred experience for them is to hear their native language spoken well.

Further, there are additional resources teachers can use that assist students' language development. For example, today there are more translators hired by school districts to assist teachers in communicating with more of their students and the students' families, and teachers could elicit the help of these translators more often than they do. There are also many more excellent books, tape recordings, and software programs in many languages designed specifically for English language learners in school.

Further, learning a few words and phrases in your students' native language can go a long way toward welcoming your students and assisting them in beginning to learn to "do school." Additionally, teachers should be encouraged when English language learners translate for one another and speak about content in their native tongues prior to attempting academic talk in English.

Most important, though, is the attitude teachers have about students and their first languages. We can learn to respect and celebrate these learners as multilingual students and recognize the gifts they bring to the classroom. Indeed, at times, the ELLs can be used as resources for native English speakers who are learning new languages, while the ELLs develop both their native tongues and English.

Reading Instruction and ELLs

Much has been written about the importance of excellent early reading instruction. Today, most educators agree that students need a balance of authentic literacy experiences with rich literature and explicit teaching of skills in a systematic manner. Indeed, the report of the National Reading Panel (NRP; NICHD, 2000) revealed *five components* of effective reading programs: phonemic awareness, phonics, reading fluency, vocabulary, and reading comprehension. *Developing Literacy in Second-Language Learners: Report of the National Literacy Panel on Language Minority Children and Youth* (August & Shanahan, 2006a) emphasizes that ELLs need "enhanced teaching of what is good for native-language speakers" (p. 16). That is, "instruction must address [the five components] *while* fostering extensive oral English language development" (p. 16). The examples we present of reading instruction in elementary classrooms emphasize the NRP components through the CREDE pedagogy. The following two examples illustrate how these two sets of standards can be woven into a week-long lesson sequence in elementary classrooms serving diverse populations, some of whom are English language learners. We begin with an example from Georgia's second-grade classroom, followed by one from Mary's third-grade classroom.

Georgia's Second Grade

This five-day lesson sequence was designed and implemented in a second-grade classroom serving poor, working class, and middle class children, a few of whom are ELLs. The teacher, Georgia, was focusing instruction on helping her young children understand issues of discrimination in a unit she calls "Who Says We Can't?" The following table includes the activities she used, the reading components from the National Reading Panel, and the CREDE standards for pedagogy. She also provided additional supports for her English language learners. Each lesson was designed to last 30–60 minutes, depending on the activity and the size of the group, and she moved in and out of whole-group and small-group instruction across the lesson sequence.

Table 5.1   Reading Instruction in Georgia's Second-Grade Classroom

Activities	NRP Reading Components	CREDE Pedagogy Standards	Notes
Day 1			
• Teacher taps into students' background knowledge before reading the story by asking the students to write two things in their Response Journals: 1) Write about a time you felt you weren't being treated fairly. 2) What can girls do during play that boys can't? What can boys do that girls can't? Why/why not? • Students share responses in pairs, then 2–3 volunteers share with whole group. • Teacher introduces new vocabulary. • Teacher & students participate in a shared reading of the story *Just Like Josh Gibson* (Johnson & Beck, 2007), with teacher guiding students in an Instructional Conversation about the meanings of the text, connecting to journal texts just shared.	Vocabulary Comprehension Writing	Contextualization Language Development Rigorous Curriculum Instructional Conversation	• Vocabulary will be reviewed a second time for small group of ELL students following the lesson.

Table 5.2   Day 2 in Georgia's Classrooom

Activities	NRP Reading Components	CREDE Pedagogy Standards	Notes
Day 2			
• Students listen to same story (*Just Like Josh Gibson*) on audiotape as they follow along with own copy of story. • Teacher leads students in choral readings of favorite passages. • Teacher reviews long vowel patterns from a previous lesson and students use the book to search for phonics patterns (e.g., vowel teams, vowel-consonant-vowel open-syllable) and then write them in correct categories on handout. • Class gathers as whole group and shares and charts words (on class chart) found in the book or other words that fit these patterns not found in the story. • Students asked to explain how they know that word follows that pattern.	Fluency Phonics	Language Development Rigorous Curriculum	• Teacher provides a few minutes of extra fluency practice for students who need it, saying the sounds slowly and explicitly. • Teacher will attend to pronunciation differences for ELLs (e.g., allowing differences in phonics learning). A tape recording of the book is made available for further listening in literacy center.

Table 5.3 Day 3 in Georgia's Classroom

Activities	NRP Reading Components	CREDE Pedagogy Standards	Notes
Day 3			
• Teacher reviews concepts and vocabulary discussed from Day 1. • Using multiple copies of the story read the day before, the students reread the story with a predetermined partner (ELLs with native English speakers), and then answer specified open-ended questions (written on handout) to require them to think more deeply about the story content. • Teacher reads with a small group to work on fluency through choral reading. • After the reading, teacher assists same group with the questions on handout—discussing their responses first and then allowing them to write responses on the handout. • The teacher meets with one group for Instructional Conversation on the meanings of the book.	Fluency Vocabulary Comprehension Writing	Contextualization Language Development Rigorous Curriculum Instructional Conversation	• Review vocabulary. • Assist students with reading by making sure they are all following along. • Rephrase questions or give choices as needed for ELL students.

Table 5.4   Day 4 in Georgia's Classroom

Activities	NRP Reading Components	CREDE Pedagogy Standards	Notes
Day 4			
• Teacher uses an 'Anticipation Guide' (Allen, 2004) to introduce new related story (*Oliver Button Is a Sissy* [de Paola, 1979]), and she leads students in a brief picture walk. • Teacher reads aloud the story. Teacher and students discuss meaning of text and why boys/girls are treated differently through Instructional Conversation. Teacher invites students to discuss in small groups these questions: (1) Should boys/girls be treated differently? (2) Why/why not? Volunteers share with whole group. • Students write their thoughts/ideas in their Response Journals. • Several share aloud their thoughts. Discuss the importance of treating others with respect.	Comprehension Fluency Writing	Conversation	• The teacher finds an extra ten minutes to meet with ELLs for further oral language time discuss the book. She assists, where needed, with vocabulary review or using sentence starters to help students discuss the views of the book.

Table 5.5   Day 5 in Georgia's Classroom

Activities	NRP Reading Components	CREDE Pedagogy Standards	Notes
Day 5			
• Teacher revisits the book *A Story of Ruby Bridges* (Coles, 2004), read earlier in the month (related book). • Teacher builds on students' experiences by asking if they were the first in their family to achieve a specific goal (teacher gives examples). • Children are provided the three books to reread during Center time. Then, teacher introduces the beginning of a small research project (which may take several lessons). She provides resources for students to work in small groups of 3–4 to research American firsts—African American, Asian American, Hispanic American, and women, completing the form provided. • Several share aloud their thoughts. Discuss the importance of treating others with respect. • Students and teacher create a timeline for their American Firsts and then examine the timelines. • Students reflect in Response Journals about whether or not they think boys/girls or different ethnic groups are still being treated this way. They must explain their thinking. • Teacher will also pose the question "How can you make a difference?" for later reader response writing.	Writing Comprehension	Joint Productive Activity Contextualization Language Development Rigorous Curriculum Instructional Conversation	• Teacher assists students with Internet work and other research skills, as needed.

As you can see, it is not always necessary or appropriate to include all CREDE standards in one lesson simply because some lessons last only 30 minutes, and a good Instructional Conversation can take an entire half hour. Many teachers think in terms of lesson sequences, in which several lessons are used to teach a particular set of concepts and skills, which makes thinking about the CREDE five standards for pedagogy a bit more manageable for teachers.

In addition to the teaching of a lesson sequence such as the one above, many teachers (perhaps Georgia, too) also provide daily, systematic phonics instruction that is not only related to the books being read this week but also built on previous phonological skills. Many students, including some English language learners, need intensive, daily phonics during their primary grade years. Of course, phonics instruction is a bit different for ELLs because there is much more focus on learning patterns of spelling and less on a standard way of pronouncing words.

Below are details of two of the strategies Georgia used in her lesson sequence above.

Anticipation Guide

An Anticipation Guide (Allen, 2004) is a reading comprehension strategy appropriate for all students, but particularly useful for English language learners. Before introducing a new book, the teacher asks students to predict what it will be about. She also invites students to answer a teacher-created quiz or survey about the topic in which students agree or disagree with certain statements. For example, for the book in Georgia's lesson, the teacher might ask students to agree with the following statement:

> Baseball is for boys.
> Dolls are for girls.

The students share their survey responses in small groups and debate their answers. Then, the book is read and discussed and the students can retake the quiz or survey and see if their opinions have changed. It is a powerful comprehension tool that not only sets the reader up to predict and connect but also helps students understand that written text can change our minds about the way we see the world.

American "Firsts" Question Form

What is the name of this famous person?
What was he or she the first to do?
When did this person live?
When did this person become the "first"?
What country did this person live in?
What is another interesting fact about this person?

Mary's Third Grade

The following lesson sequence was designed for third-grade students, and it is focused on women in history. Like Georgia, Mary's goal was to weave the five components of the NRP report with the five standards of CREDE. Additionally, Mary's "Notes" to herself indicate her plans to focus her teaching on equitable turn taking, wait time, and feedback during discussions (Ferguson, 1998).

Table 5.6   Reading Instructions in Mary's Third-Grade Classroom

Activities	Reading Components	Pedagogy Standards	Notes
Day 1			
• Teacher introduces and discusses the importance of reading about women and their contribution to history. With multiple copies of *Maya Lin Linking People and Places* (Scraper, 2005), the teacher guides the students in previewing the book, noting its genre and organizational structure. Teacher reads aloud pp. 1–5, discussing vocabulary in context. Pairs of students then complete the reading of the text to find out the results of the competition. • At whole-group share time, teacher has students reread Maya's quote on p. 6 and leads an Instructional Conversation.	Comprehension Vocabulary Fluency	Language Development Rigorous Curriculum Instructional Conversation	• Attention is paid to equitable participation, partner selection, and discourse structures during discussion. • Teacher leads ELL students in a word sort activity, later using the vocabulary from the story.

Table 5.7   Day 2 in Mary's Classroom

Activities	Reading Components	Pedagogy Standards	Notes
Day 2			
• Teacher leads students in a word sort activity using vocabulary words found in the text. Students sort them into groups based on similarities. Students share/discuss their groupings. Pairs of students reread pp. 15–17 of *Maya Lin Linking People and Places* and discuss the Women's Table sculpture and its significance. Students come together in a whole-group setting to discuss this sculpture's symbolism and impact on the equitable treatment of women.	Vocabulary Phonics Fluency Comprehension	Instructional Conversation Rigorous Curriculum	• Language Development • Attention is paid to equitable participation, partner selection, and discourse structures during discussion. ELLs will be encouraged to work with native English speakers for the word sort activity.

Table 5.8   Days 3 and 4 in Mary's Classroom

Activities	Reading Components	Pedagogy Standards	Notes
Day 3			
• Teacher shares an interactive Web site featuring women in an electronic quotable wall of portraits entitled "Women's Words of Wisdom: Thoughts Over Time." Teacher guides students in a discussion on the impact of each of these women's lives and how they have affected our lives. http://memory.loc.gov/learn/features/womenswords/	Comprehension	Contextualization Instructional Conversation Rigorous Curriculum	• Attention is paid to equitable participation, partner selection, and discourse structures during discussion. • The teacher spends an additional 10–15 minutes with ELLs for extra oral language development time, repeating the discussion of the Web site materials.
Day 4			
• Students are grouped to research a woman from history using the Internet. Groups will create a portrait of their subject with a direct quote or one she may have said, based on their readings. Students will also write a short summary of the important contributions made by their subject. Portraits with quotes and summaries will be used to create a class "Women's Words of Wisdom" to be displayed on the bulletin board in the hallway.	Comprehension	Joint Productive Activity Rigorous Curriculum Language Development	• Attention is paid to equitable participation, group selection, and discourse structures during discussion. • Scribes for ELLs and other identified students will be available, if needed.

Table 5.9   Day 5 in Mary's Classroom

Activities	Reading Components	Pedagogy Standards	Notes
Day 5			
• Students will share their portraits, quotes, and summaries with the whole group in an oral presentation. Following each presentation, the teacher will guide an Instructional Conversation on why these women have been so successful and what barriers they may have overcome. Students will also discuss the significance of the quotes selected for display.	Comprehension	Joint Productive Activity Rigorous Curriculum Language Development	• Attention is paid to equitable participation, group selection, and discourse structures during discussion. • Scribes for identified students will be available.

As you can see, both elementary teachers also connect writing to reading in their lessons. They understand that writing shapes thinking and that students can come to new understandings as they write. This process is also understood by Jayne, middle school ESL teacher, whose students are still in the early stages of learning English.

Writing in Middle School

As a culminating activity after reading the novel *Esperanza Rising* (Ryan, 2002), Jayne wanted her sixth-grade students to create a three-dimensional project—either a standing cube, a diorama, or an accordion book—in which they summarized and illustrated the plot and some of their favorite scenes from the novel. Because many of her students are recent immigrants, Jayne knew the students would need help writing their summaries, so she reviewed with them how to use the Somebody Wanted But So (SWBS) strategy from Kylene Beers's book, *When Kids Can't Read: What Teachers Can Do* (2002).

Although they had used this strategy earlier in the year, she knew a quick review would help. So Jayne began with whole-class instruction; using her laptop and projector, she and the students together created a graphic organizer based on the familiar story of "The Three Little Pigs".

Table 5.10   Graphic Organizer for Writing

Somebody (Main Character)	Wanted	But (Conflict)	So (Resolution)
The three little pigs	to build a house for themselves	each time they did, the wolf huffed and he puffed and he blew the house down	the pigs finally built a house of bricks and the wolf couldn't blow it down. He tried to climb down the chimney and he fell in the pot of boiling water and died.

Next, Jayne paired up the students with their project partner and told them, "Now, we're going to create another Somebody Wanted But So chart, but this time, it will be for Esperanza." She said to them, "Go ahead and make another four-column chart in your class notebook, just like we did before, and then we'll talk about what to do next. You need only one chart, so decide which of you is going to do the writing for now." Once the students had discussed their roles and created their four-column chart, Jayne started them off by asking, "OK, who would be the 'somebody' in our chart?"

"Esperanza!" called out several students.

"Right! So let's put Esperanza in the Somebody column. Now, what did Esperanza want? Think about this, and talk about it with your partner. Then, try to write one or two sentences in the Wanted column that tell what Esperanza wanted." Jayne felt that this was a pivotal point in the lesson because, although she and the students could have continued working together to create a Somebody Wanted But So chart as a whole class, Jayne deliberately moved from whole-class to partner work. Jayne wanted the students to begin thinking on their own, and she wanted them to have the opportunity to express their individual perspectives on the novel.

As students began talking and conferring together, Jayne walked around and encouraged and guided them. In doing this, she noticed that several groups were focusing on some of the minor details of the novel, rather than on the overall plot. To help refocus them, she asked one group, "OK, you're talking about one thing that Esperanza wanted—to have her Abuelita come to California—but is that really the main focus of the novel? Is that the big picture?"

The students thought about it and said, "No, not really."

"OK, then think about the big picture idea here. What did Esperanza want more than anything?"

"To stay rich?" said one student.

"Right! She really wanted her life to stay the way it was before her Papa died, didn't she? So try to write a couple of sentences focused on that."

As students continued to work together to create their charts focusing on the problem and solution to the novel, Jayne continued to circulate. Because students were seated at round tables, with three or four students at each table, she was able to sit down and talk with several different groups, assessing their progress and providing support when students were struggling with an aspect of the activity. By the end of this part of the lesson, each pair of students had created their own SWBS chart—none of the charts were exactly alike, but each summarized the overall plot of the novel, *Esperanza Rising*. For the next class period, students were able to move from creating a SWBS chart about the plot to choosing two scenes from the novel that they and their partner especially enjoyed and summarizing them. Students then took each of their SWBS charts and, with some guidance from Jayne, were able to transform them into paragraphs, which they typed out and used as part of their projects.

Writing Across the Curriculum

As stated earlier, writing shapes thinking in the same ways that talking does, especially when students write to understand. For a few examples, teachers we have known have asked students to do the following:

- Write about what the number ten means.
- Write the process (steps) for figuring out a division problem.

- Create mathematics word problems using everyday circumstances.
- Explain the water cycle using words and pictures.
- Keep a journal reflecting on what was learned in science or social studies classes.
- Write pros and cons for a fictitious war.

Tips for Language and Literacy Teaching

- Weave all five CREDE components into any given lesson, where appropriate. JPA provides opportunity for academic language (CALP) peer interaction and thus opportunities for language development.
- Have students write questions they think a teacher will ask them about a story or nonfiction text before they read the text. Have them add questions they think a teacher would ask after reading the selection. Then, students compare their questions to those the teacher does ask. Over time, question asking becomes a sort of Anticipation Guide (Allen, 2004).
- Have students write about what they are learning in mathematics, science, and social studies as well as in their language arts classes, such as the examples above.
- Good questioning techniques lead to opportunities for oral language development. See Chapter 6 for ways to move toward excellent questioning.
- Plan a few minutes of extra time for your English language learners for oral language development/ concept review time. Even ten additional minutes talking about the previous lesson can help students move from "sort of understanding" to fully understanding.

Assessing Your Teaching of Language and Literacy

The following questions can help you monitor your implementation of the CREDE language and literacy standard:

1. Do I listen to students talk about familiar topics such as home and community?

2. Do I respond to students' talk and questions, making 'in-flight' changes during conversation that directly relate to students' comments?

3. Do I assist written and oral language development through modeling, eliciting, probing, restating, clarifying, questioning, praising, and so on, in purposeful conversation and writing?

4. Do I interact with students in ways that respect students' preferences for speaking that may be different from the teacher's, such as wait-time, eye contact, turn taking, or spotlighting?

5. Do I connect student language with literacy and content area knowledge through speaking, listening, reading, and writing activities?

6. Do I encourage students to use content vocabulary to express their understanding?

7. Do I provide frequent opportunity for students to interact with one another and the teacher during instructional activities?

8. Do I encourage students' use of first and second languages in instructional activities?

These assessment indicators do not include all of what is critical for the teaching of reading and writing (see the earlier parts of the chapter for more on this); however, these questions will guide you to knowing whether you are allowing the kind of oral language development and literacy practice that is necessary. Implementation of this standard indicates your overall respect you have for your students, their experiences, and language.

6

Engaging Students With Rigorous Curriculum

High Expectations for English Language Learners

The education of English language learners has evolved immensely over the last few decades, and most of the changes have been positive. Today, many school districts offer both ESL and mainstream classroom settings for ELLs, others offer bilingual education, and still others offer extra support outside the regular classroom for ELLs. We applaud these changes.

However, there is evidence that in many places, especially in school districts relatively new to serving large populations of ELLs, educators still hold deficit views of these students. Some seem to believe that if a student's English is not polished, it is an indicator of the student's learning abilities. Others may assume that if students come from poorer countries, their academic skills must be lacking. Some believe that a "basics" curriculum is key to helping ELLs develop. We have observed instances in which English language learners are put into ESL classrooms that focus only on "survival skills," such as reading food labels, rather than on the science, mathematics, and social studies curriculum the students want and need. We have heard about ELLs being shuffled into special education classes even though they may not have learning disabilities.

Our view is that English language learners are as capable of learning the academic curriculum as is any other group. It may mean that these students need extra support, extra time learning academic English, and possibly a review of the "basic skills" that serve as the foundation for learning content. However, we also believe it essential that students be exposed, with support, to the academic content of their peers. We believe it essential that all students, including ELLs, are scaffolded to learn a rigorous curriculum.

What, then, does a rigorous curriculum look like when enacted in classrooms? Instruction that requires students to think deeply and strategically about what they are learning is key. Certainly, students need to know rules (phonics, math facts, historical events, and scientific procedures), but, more important, they need to learn how to analyze and use the content they are learning in meaningful applications. Students need lessons that require them to stretch, but not so much that they become discouraged.

This book has already illustrated several examples of teachers with high expectations who implement a rigorous curriculum. Cori used history to help her students grapple with big ideas about why and how cities develop. In doing so, she helped students connect the tragedy of Katrina to scientific concepts. Justin taught his students about racism among soldiers during the Vietnam War, a topic that many students could connect with today's war in Iraq and the many students of color who serve in that war. Vickie asked her students to try to see with writers' eyes, and they searched for and produced text that "shows" and does not "tell." The effective ELL teacher not only presents content at a high level but also works to find strategies to support students' attempts at this work. This chapter will provide examples of high-level learning accompanied by scaffolds that support the learning.

Adapting Instruction to Maintain Rigor and Provide Support

One of the most effective strategies for maintaining rigorous curriculum for English language learners is to adapt the grade-appropriate materials you are teaching so that they are accessible for ELLs. For example, recently in Jayne's classroom the students faced the challenge of writing a reflective essay for their state-assessed writing portfolio. The *Kentucky Core Content for Assessment v. 4.1* prescribed the focus of the essay: "For the Writing Portfolio Assessment, the reflective piece must have as its central focus growth in writing through the lens of literacy" (Kentucky Department of Education, 2008, p. 81).

One of the most challenging academic skills for ELLs to develop is writing. In general, their speaking and reading skills will progress at a faster pace than their writing skills, and even when an ELL is on grade level for speaking, listening, and reading, his or her writing skills quite often lag behind. Writing well is a skill that is challenging for native speakers of a language. Imagine the challenge of learning to write well in a second language! So, how does one begin?

The first step is to adapt materials you are using to make them accessible to ELLs. For example, to begin this unit on reflective writing, Jayne provided students with several reflective writing pieces as examples. The first was from the text *Speaking of Reading*, by Nadine Rosenthal (1995). From this text Jayne copied a short reflective essay by Isabel Allende in which she reflects on some of the significant events in her own literacy history. Although Jayne knew that she wanted to use this piece because of its rich language and depth of reflection, she also knew that it would be a challenge for some of the ELLs in her classroom.

Jayne decided to annotate the text by underlining the challenging vocabulary and providing a glossary of short definitions or synonyms for these words right on each page of the text. Next, she identified the *essential question* she wanted the students to focus on as they read the text and printed the question on the top of the page. She realized that, even with the glossary, the students still would not fully comprehend some things as they read the piece, which is the true purpose of the lesson. Providing them with an essential question assisted the students in refining and narrowing their focus to one particular aspect of the text rather than having to read and comprehend the entire piece.

Jayne used the same technique of identifying and glossing challenging vocabulary along with identifying an essential question with the two other examples they were going to read together. These included another selection from *Speaking of Reading* and a selection from *The Struggle to Be Strong*—"How Writing Helps Me," an essay written by a sixteen-year-old named Terry Ann Da Costa

(2000). She believed that with these three pieces, the students would have a good foundational understanding of the type of reflection they needed to do.

Next, Jayne had her students read the text aloud in pairs. Having students read with a partner provides wonderful opportunities for student interaction and relationship building, since you can pair stronger and weaker students together, or an ELL with a native speaker, or simply give two students who work well together the opportunity to interact. As the students read, Jayne instructed them to listen to their partner and, if the partner seemed to stumble or hesitate, to jump right in and help him or her pronounce unfamiliar words.

Once the partners had finished reading the text together, she asked the students to read the text again, this time silently to themselves, using the INSERT (Interactive Notation System for Effective Reading and Thinking) reading strategy (Vaughn & Estes, 1986). This strategy requires students to code text with the following notations as they read:

X	I thought differently
+	New information
!!!	Wow/very important
??	I don't understand
=	This reminds me of something

Jayne has a chart hanging on the wall in her classroom and bookmarks for the students to use to help them implement this strategy. The students have used this strategy often enough that they know that as they read, they are to interact with the text by marking places where they learn new information (+), where they find something very important (!!!), where they make connections (=), and so on. Before they started this silent reading, Jayne reminded them that their focus was not to understand the entire text but to answer the essential question written at the top of the first page. Using this system of (1) annotation, (2) glossing, and (3) identifying a purpose for reading through identification of an essential question allowed even struggling English language learners to interact with the text. This approach maintained the rigor of the content for the students without the frustration that often results with trying to decipher text that is a bit beyond their instructional reading level.

When the students had read this text twice, Jayne was ready for them to link their reading to writing. First, she asked them to get out their writer's notebook and answer the essential question she had asked, referring back to the text and their INSERT strategy coding as they wrote. For the Allende text, her essential question was, "What metaphors and similes does Allende use to describe her relationship with reading and writing? What metaphors and similes describe your relationship with reading and writing?" Although at this point Jayne could have gone right from reading to discussion, she knew that ELLs often need time to think things out by writing them down, so she wanted to provide the students the opportunity to clarify their thinking through writing. Allowing them to write out their thoughts provided a verbal scaffold for them to refer to during small-group discussion. During the discussion they either read exactly what they had written or summarized what they wrote. They were not put in the uncomfortable position of having to spontaneously think *and* speak in a second language, which so often causes students to panic and then have nothing to contribute. After the students spent five minutes or so organizing their thoughts, they were ready for small-group discussion.

During the discussion, students not only were able to clarify their own understanding of the text further but also were exposed to the thoughts and ideas of the other students. As the students discussed, Jayne circulated throughout the room, listening and noting students who needed a little more help with understanding. Finally, she asked the students to reread their initial writer's notebook entry response to the essential question and then revise and add to it, using some of the ideas they had gleaned from their small-group discussions of the text. This writer's notebook entry could then later be incorporated into their reflective essay.

This lesson demonstrates the characteristics of a rigorous curriculum, as described below. However, it also shows Jayne building from what students have learned previously (see Chapter 4), focuses on language and literacy experiences (see Chapter 5), and provides an opportunity for joint productive activity (see Chapter 3) in the students' small-group discussion. We can also see that the structure is in place for Jayne to conduct an Instructional Conversation (see Chapter 7).

Meaning of Rigorous Curriculum

Sometimes well-intentioned teachers make such comments as "My students have been in the United States for only a few months, so I'm not focusing much on content. I just want them to practice their English right now," or "When I assess my English language learners, I overlook a lot of their mistakes so they don't get discouraged." While these views at first seem supportive and kind, this type of benign neglect about performance can, in fact, put such students at even greater risk of educational failure. Instead, teachers need to set high academic standards for these students and to assess in ways that offer not only feedback but also helpful support in correcting students' misunderstandings and errors.

We all know (no doubt from our own schooling experiences) how lessons that do not challenge students look and feel—boring, boring, boring. They lack meaningfulness, are often disjointed from other lessons, provide little opportunity to address or pose significant questions, and leave no lasting impact other than bad memories.

Teaching a rigorous curriculum that engages students in reaching high standards requires certain essential components. Teachers must have a sense of the goals they want their students to achieve, and these goals must be developmentally appropriate and attainable. Jayne and Johanna teach in a state that has established, through extensive collaborations of teachers and state education personnel, programs of study and core content for assessment. They can use these frameworks to derive their instructional goals, knowing that they have been carefully designed by their peers and other experts.

In addition, teachers must know their students' starting points in learning the content. Ongoing, informal, and at times more formal assessments can help teachers figure out the next steps to take in their teaching, as well as what differentiations might be necessary based on students' varied needs. This is especially necessary when working with English language learners who are new to U.S. schools, the content, and the language. Small-group instruction, such as what Jayne used, provides a way for teachers to assess by listening as students discuss the work and intervening, if needed, to correct misunderstandings, clarify expectations, or to redirect students' focus on the task at hand.

Further, teachers must be skilled in designing instructional strategies that can help students work in their zone of proximal development (Vygotsky, 1978) and ultimately reach the expected high academic standards. Expert and effective teachers know how to nudge students and, at the same time, provide the scaffolding needed along the way toward new understandings. Note, for example, how Jayne provided such assistance through the use of examples, annotated text, essential questions to guide students' reading, and a previously taught reading strategy that was also visible in the room.

Those writing about culturally responsive teaching reiterate similar points about the need to maintain high expectations for students and not "dummy down" the curriculum while at the same time providing the support needed for learning (Delpit, 1995; Ladson-Billings, 1994; McIntyre, Rosebery, & González, 2001; Moll, 1992; Tharp et al., 2000; Tharp & Gallimore, 1988). Such expectations must be maintained for English language learners, who all too often are assumed to have limited ability because of their limited command of their new language. Indeed, in some classrooms, these students are physically put aside to work on skill-and-drill worksheets while the teachers engage the native English speakers in more cognitively rich activities and discussions. Over time, the accumulation of such experiences causes English language learners to fall further and further behind in their understanding of academic content and, as a result, in their ability to become the most productive and contributing citizens possible. In addition, such isolation restricts the students' opportunities to engage in the language experiences they need to become more capable English speakers, readers, and writers. One of the benefits of the No Child Left Behind legislation is the disaggregation of achievement data, which makes the performance of ELLs more visible and the need for instructional changes more apparent.

Still Important: Levels of Questioning

Teachers familiar with Bloom's taxonomy (1984) add rigor to their lessons by asking more questions that require students to analyze, synthesize, and evaluate what they are learning rather than the more typical, lower-level, "who, when, where?" knowledge kinds of questions. (More on Bloom's taxonomy is in Chapter 7.) Jayne, for instance, challenged her students not only to analyze the metaphors and similes Allende uses in her writing to describe her relationship with reading and writing but also to evaluate them by comparing their own metaphors and similes about reading and writing to the author's.

Teaching in this way is no small feat for a teacher. As Tharp et al. (2000) note, "It is much easier to teach to routine, minimum standards, because challenging students toward cognitive growth requires that teachers challenge, assess, and assist themselves right along with the learners (p. 30)." After considering what teachers in general do to make their curriculum more rigorous, we "visit" the classrooms of Jayne and Johanna to see how they put such lessons into practice with their students.

Indicators of Rigorous Curriculum

The Center for Research on Education, Diversity, and Excellence (CREDE) suggests five indicators of instruction that promote cognitive challenge and growth for students (http://crede.berkeley.edu/standards/3cont.shtml).

Indicators of Rigorous Curriculum

The teacher

- ensures that—for each instructional topic—students see the whole picture as a basis for understanding the parts.
- presents challenging standards for student performance.
- designs instructional tasks that advance student understanding to more complex levels.
- assists students to accomplish more complex understanding by building from their previous success.
- gives clear, direct feedback about how student performance compares with the challenging standards.

Examples of Rigorous Curriculum

In the following examples, we see how Johanna and Jayne challenge their kindergarten, middle school, and elementary students. As you read, keep the above indicators in mind and look for ways they are shown in these lessons.

Rigorous Curriculum Enacted in Kindergarten

Johanna's kindergarten students sit in front of her on the carpet. They know the routine well, for when Johanna asks what question they want to ask her, they chorus, "What is the objective?"

Johanna then reads the content objective from the chart. "Students will explore their own shadows and identify what is needed to produce a shadow. That means we're going to figure out what it takes to produce a shadow. And our language objective is, 'Students will identify three things needed to produce a shadow.'"

One student pipes up, "Like a shadow puppet. You can make a shadow puppet with your hands."

Johanna responds enthusiastically to this contribution. "You mean like our Groundhog Day puppets. Naya made a connection with our social studies. You brought this up before I did. Way to go! What did we learn about groundhogs?"

Gabby offers, "When they come out of the hole, they lose their shadow," and Johanna prompts, "What do they look for when they come out?" Gabby replies, "Their shadow."

Johanna notices that it's getting cloudy outside, which interferes with her original plan to go outside and have the students make shadows. She points out to the students that without the sun, making shadows is more difficult. She adjusts by moving closer to the window and, as the sun comes out briefly, having the children point out her shadow and the table's shadow that they can see on the floor.

Johanna then directs the students to the key concept for the lesson. "There are three magical ingredients we need for a shadow. Does someone know what number one is?"

Sharon suggests, "A light," and Johanna replies, "Very good. What was the light when we saw the shadows on the floor?" and the children identify the sun as the light source.

Johanna then asks, "What's something else that we need for a shadow?" and Deshaw responds, "A human." Johanna supports and modifies this response. "That's right. So, we need a *light*, and we need an *object*, which this time was a person, but we also saw the shadow of the table, another object. And we have something else… this is a really hard thing." She notices Naya looking around to find the chart where Johanna has written words about making a shadow. "Do you see what Naya is doing? He's using our *visuals*. He thought to himself, 'I'm going to use this tool up here to help me figure out the third special ingredient. Number one, we need a light or sun;

number two, we need an object..." and then she helps Shawn sound out the word *surface* written on the chart. "I'm going to help you understand what *surface* means. What did you see the shadow on?" The children identify the floor or ground, and Johanna reminds them that the *surface* is where the shadow is shown.

She then directs them to the area where she reads to them. "I have another visual to give you clues—a big book." They first take a look at the cover, identifying the sun as the light source, a fence as the object, and the snow as the surface. After a bit more reading about sources of light and the creation of shadows, Johanna introduces the word *silhouette* and shows them a silhouette. Anna identifies it as a silhouette of Abraham Lincoln, and Jackie uses the magic pointer to trace its outline. Johanna points out, "Now we're making another connection. Remember when we read this book [holding it up] about Abraham Lincoln? Look at his face on the cover. If you turn his face and shine a light, you will see his shadow. Someone has traced the outline of his shadow to make a *silhouette.* How neat is that? So, if you would like a silhouette of yourself, raise your hand...Oh, many of you do! That's what we're going to do. But, let's think about this. We need three things. One is *light.* Do we have a lot of sun today? No, so what is another source of light that we could use?"

A child volunteers "A lamp," and Johanna agrees. "Yes, we could use a lamp. And, what is our *object* going to be? Jada?"

Jada suggests "People," and Johanna says excitedly, "It's going to be *you!* You're going to be the object. And what is our surface going to be?"

Another child volunteers, "The hard floor." Johanna acknowledges that they did see shadows on the floor, but for the silhouettes, the surface will be a piece of paper.

For the next several minutes, Johanna and her assistant each take a group of children to make the silhouettes. Johanna works in the hallway but soon realizes it's too bright to make much of a shadow, even with the use of the lamp. After awhile, she suggests they go back to a darker corner of the classroom. Reminding the children that they will finish making the silhouettes tomorrow, Johanna directs the students to write in their science notebooks about the three things needed to make a shadow.

Naya, who was in the group in the hallway, says excitedly, "You need one more for the three. You need *dark.*"

Johanna smiles and agrees, "Naya brings up a great point. He said we need to add a number 4. You know what happened when we went into the hallway—it was so bright all around us that it didn't cast a shadow, did it? So, we had to come into the classroom where it was a little darker around the light so it would cast a shadow. What a great observation!" She adds *dark surrounding* to the list of what's needed to make a shadow. After reviewing the list, the children then write (or, for some, draw) in their science notebooks, and Johanna invites four to share at the end of the lesson.

Just as we observed Jayne do with her students, we can see Johanna relate the lesson to students' previous learning (see Chapter 4), focus on content vocabulary and literacy activities (see Chapter 5), and build in opportunities for students to engage in a joint productive activity (see Chapter 3). Further, Johanna provides a great deal of scaffolding for her young learners with visual cues, demonstrations, and activities that illustrate the science concepts she is teaching. The conversation with the students includes much questioning (although still more low-level at this point) and offers students the chance to make observations and connections. These observations and connections can lead to questions that make them think more deeply about ideas, important even for kindergartners. can answer questions that make them think more deeply about ideas.

Rigorous Curriculum Enacted in Middle Grades Language Arts

For a recent lesson in Jayne's classroom, she directed the students' attention to the following objective, written on the board and read aloud: "Take a stand on debatable issues and understand the importance of supporting a position with concrete reasons." These students, all English language learners, are learning much more than new words and what they mean; they are also learning how to use language for an intended purpose. This can be a distinct challenge for all students but especially for ELLs. For this task, the students must understand the situation, clarify their thinking about it, and then figure out how to articulate their reasoning in speech and, later, in writing. Although the focus in analyzing this lesson is on the rigorous curriculum that Jayne provides, the lesson just as obviously demonstrates the CREDE standard on *language and literacy* (see Chapter 5) in its focus on articulating viewpoints during role playing and on *contextualization* (see Chapter 4) in Jayne's use of familiar topics for the students' debatable issues.

Jayne begins, "I want you to think about the word *persuade.*" She hands out a sheet of paper to each student, reminding them that they have talked about this many times. On the paper, they are to write what *persuade* means. When they finish, they offer their responses.

Roberto shares, "To convince someone to do something."

Jayne writes this on the overhead and asks how many others have used the word *convince.* Many raise their hands and share that they also used words like *"make someone."* Jayne reinforces this and reminds them that we persuade others to *think or believe something* or to *act or do something.* She then connects the lesson to what the students will later need to know in order to write persuasively for on-demand writing assessments.

Jayne notes, "Everyone has opinions about everything. I have opinions. For example, I have an opinion that summer is the best time of year. Now, I can say that, but I need to be able to support my opinion with reasons. So, I am going to give you two reasons why I think summer is the best time of the year. One, I get to go on vacation. And, two, I don't have to work. Those are two good reasons to enjoy summertime. Now, someone else might think winter is the best time of the year, so they might disagree. Therefore, to persuade someone that he or she should have the same opinion as you, you have to have reasons. Today we're going to focus on the importance of supporting a position with reasons—not only having an opinion but also having reasons to support that opinion so that it's persuasive for others. What we're going to do—I'm going to read some statements to you, and I want you to think about whether you agree with the statement or you disagree."

Jayne then points out that each opposite side of the classroom has a label posted—one marked *agree,* the other marked *disagree*—to designate where the students should move to show their opinion about the statements she will read.

Jayne reminds them, "Another word for *agree* is *pro,* and another word for *disagree* is *con.* After you move, I then want you to give the reasons for your opinion."

At this point in Jayne's lesson, she has focused mostly on vocabulary rather than on ideas and concepts, a place where many teachers remain, especially with English language learners. The next part of her lesson, however, goes beyond vocabulary teaching to the *use* of the vocabulary for the discussion of ideas. In this way, Jayne has maintained middle-grades-level rigor in her lessons.

The students then listen to the first opinion listed on the over-head as Jayne reads it: "It is appropriate—it is OK—to burn an American flag in the classroom in order to motivate students to write about freedom of expression." All the students move to the *disagree* side of the room.

Jayne observes, "Everyone disagrees with that statement. Now, what reasons can you give that it is not appropriate, it is not OK, to burn an American flag?"

Amador offers his reason. "It's dangerous, because like burning, a fire can burn a person or burn the building."

Jayne responds, "OK, does that seem like a good reason?" The students agree that it does.

Jayne then asks, "Can you think of other reasons? Marianj?" She offers a quiet response about America, and Jayne offers, "You mean it's disrespectful?" and the student nods yes.

This pattern continues for the next statement, "CHAMPS [mentioned in Chapter 3] improves student behavior and reduces discipline problems in the school." At first, everyone moves to the *agree* side of the room, but Jayne encourages them not to follow the crowd and to consider what they really think. She notes, "I'd like to hear different opinions. Wouldn't you?" Amador decides to be the lone dissenter and moves across the room to stand under the *disagree* sign.

Amador shares his view. "Not all schools use it, and they have other ways for behavior and discipline."

Convinced by his reason, another student moves across the room to stand next to him and offers another view. "I think like CHAMPS works inside a class but not outside in the school where they [students] don't change."

More demonstrations continue in response to the statements "Students learn and perform better academically in single-gender, all-boy or all-girl classrooms" and "Middle school students should be required to take a daily physical education class." Jayne scaffolds the students' responses by pointing out that they are using their own and others' experiences as well as good reasons to support their opinions.

Following the active engagement of the students in showing and then verbalizing the reasons for their opinions, Jayne makes the transition to a writing activity. After all, preparing the students well for the persuasive writing they will eventually need to produce has been the purpose of these demonstrations and discussions. Now, she asks them to "take a stand" in a letter or speech in response to one of several prompts, requiring them to support their opinions with reasons and examples. Her assessment then focuses on how well they are meeting the expectation of writing in a more persuasive way.

Reflection on Examples

Across the above examples, we see how both teachers challenged their students, including the many English language learners they teach. By focusing attention on each lesson's content and language objectives, they helped the students see the "whole picture" of the content, whether it was science concepts about light or literacy concepts about reflective writing and persuasive language.

The teachers also let students know what kinds of work and performances were expected of them in order to achieve the objectives, and they challenged the students to reach high standards. Johanna's kindergarten students knew they had to learn how to "identify what is needed to produce a shadow," and Jayne's middle schoolers faced the challenge of figuring out how to "take a stand on debatable issues and understand the importance of supporting a position with concrete reasons."

Further, the teachers provided scaffolds instructionally to help the students develop complex understandings of the concepts. Jayne and Johanna did not "water down" the vocabulary needed for learning, but instead engaged the students actively in exploring the meanings of new words and ideas.

Although the concepts and vocabulary might be an educational "stretch" for the students, especially those who are just learning English, the key is the kind of teaching taking place in these classrooms. In each setting, the teacher builds from the students' previous success, experience, and understanding and, in doing so, makes the learning more comprehensible.

Further, across all examples, we see how implementing a rigorous curriculum is more easily accomplished with the integration of other CREDE standards as well. For instance, engaging the students in rich *language and literacy* (see Chapter 5) events occurs in all of these classrooms, especially as those events are *contextualized* (see Chapter 4) in students' prior experiences and involve meaningful *joint productive activities* (see Chapter 3). Although the lessons do not illustrate a planned Instructional Conversation as defined by CREDE (see Chapter 7), each teacher has established the structure and routines in the classroom for this to happen. In order to accomplish what these teachers have done, the following questions can be useful guides for planning.

Questions to Guide Planning

- In examining the curriculum frameworks in your context, consider the following questions: Which of these goals would be the easiest for my English language learners to attain? Which would be the most difficult and require more scaffolding?
- Focus on determining what students know and are able to do related to the academic goals. Consider such questions as: How can I best assess students' beginning understandings and skills? What do these assessments help me know about what I need to plan and provide in my lessons? What resources do I need for those lessons?
- Explore a range of instructional strategies that can challenge all students yet provide needed support at the same time. Pose questions such as these: In what ways can I make the expected outcomes of what's to be learned explicit for the students? How can I vary the grouping patterns so that students can learn from others as well as from me? How can I actively involve students in problem-solving experiences and collaborative projects? How can I structure the classroom activities so that I have times to engage small groups of students in intentional discussions about their learning? What would help the students become better able to assess their own learning?

Teaching Tips for Rigorous Curriculum

- Be explicit about the lesson's objectives.
- Make clear the high standards for performance.
- Ask questions that focus more on application, analysis, synthesis, and evaluation than on knowledge and comprehension.
- Plan authentic problem-solving activities that are meaningful for the students.
- Organize students in varied grouping patterns so that they can assist one another in learning the concepts.
- Plan enough time to interact with small groups so that sustained dialogue can occur about the content.

- Ask open-ended questions that give students a chance to share their thinking.
- Offer opportunities for students to pose questions.
- Use inaccurate or incomplete student responses as an opportunity for teaching.
- Scaffold students' learning through graphic organizers, use of media, real materials, role-playing, and so on.
- Incorporate varied ways to assess students' understandings.
- Display and celebrate the products and other outcomes of students' work.
- Engage students in assessments of their own learning and of group processes.

Assessing Whether Your Curriculum Is Rigorous

Assessing whether your curriculum is rigorous may perhaps be the most difficult of the CREDE standards to monitor. It takes knowing your students well—their strengths and areas of growth. It takes assessing their oral and print language levels as well as the content they know. Done well, it means teaching in students' zones of proximal development—that place in their development in which they can successfully accomplish an academic task with help, but may not be able to do so independently. The following questions, developed from CREDE, can lead you to begin thinking about what is "just right" teaching for your students.

1. Do I ensure that my students see the "whole picture" as a basis for understanding the parts?

2. Do I present challenging standards for student performance to my students?

3. Do I design instructional tasks that advance student understanding to more complex levels?

4. Do I assist students to accomplish more complex understanding by building from their previous success?

5. Do I give clear, direct feedback about how student performance compares with the challenging standards?

7

Instructional Conversation (IC)

Georgia is meeting with seven students from her second-grade class. She is discussing with them the book the class has just finished reading, *Oliver Button Is a Sissy* (de Paola, 1979), in which a young boy is picked on because what he likes to do (i.e., dance) is perceived by some of the kids as "for girls only." Georgia says to the students, "Show me thumbs up or down if you think Oliver was being discriminated against. Thumbs up if you think so." All thumbs go up in agreement. Georgia then says, "Now think about *how* Oliver is discriminated against." As hands begin to shoot up to be called on, Georgia stops the children and says, "Take a moment and just think about what you would say." The students become quiet. After a minute or so, Georgia says to the students, "Turn to your partner and explain *how* Oliver is being discriminated against."

As the students begin to talk, Georgia moves to one pair of students and participates in their conversation. The boy says, "When I was three I played with girl things, but then some older boys started picking on me. So someone was going to get hurt."

The girl responds, "That's what happens when kids tease—someone gets hurt."

Georgia asks the student, "Did you quit playing with those things because you were getting picked on?"

The boy thinks a moment. "Um, no, I quit because they were, like, baby things."

Georgia responds, "You grew out of it."

The girl says, "It's like a snake shedding its skin."

This snippet of a classroom dialogue is known as an Instructional Conversation (Dalton, 2007; Goldenberg, 1993; Tharp & Gallimore, 1988) and it differs from standard classroom discussion in that it is a structured way of scaffolding students' understandings. This final CREDE standard begins with teachers setting a goal about the content they want students to learn through the dialogic lesson. In the above lesson, which was part of Georgia's unit on discrimination described in Chapter 5, the goal was to help students understand concepts of gender discrimination. The Instructional Conversation (IC) is always contextualized in what students already know, provides much time for language development, and is highly rigorous. It may lead to joint productive activity or it may extend from it. In this way, the Instructional Conversation brings together all the CREDE standards.

Rationale and Definition of Instructional Conversation

Two researchers (Saunders & Goldenberg, 1999) who have studied the effects of Instructional Conversations (IC) on English language learners in classrooms define ICs as follows:

> Teacher and students engage in discussion about something that matters to the participants, has a coherent and discernible focus, involves a high level of participation, allows teacher and students to explore ideas and thoughts in depth, and ultimately helps students arrive at higher levels of understanding about topics under discussion (e.g., content, themes, and personal experiences related to a story). (p. 142)

These researchers found that when teachers implemented ICs with English language learners, the learners acquired deeper understandings of the topics discussed. They also found that students' oral language improved with the increased opportunities for academic talk.

How Does IC Differ From Traditional Teaching?

For many teachers, it is still a mystery how to get children to participate in discussions around literature in ways that move away from traditional classroom discourse toward more authentic discussion. Traditional classroom discourse—in which the teacher asks all the questions, does most of the talking, and takes a turn between students' responses (Cazden, 1988)—is what most of us have experienced throughout our schooling. Thus, breaking out of this habit is a huge struggle for teachers. Some teachers have tried literature circles, but gave up when they saw wasted time or phony conversations. In a study of teachers implementing the five CREDE standards (McIntyre et al., 2006), teachers claimed that implementing the Instructional Conversation (IC) was the most difficult of the standards. Teachers seem hard-wired to ask questions, wait for a student to answer the question (usually with one word or a short phrase), and then evaluate the response in some way (e.g., "Good! Correct!"). But this form of talk is extremely limiting for students because so little talk is actually done by the students. It is most detrimental to English language learners because they need many opportunities to practice speaking about ideas. How can teachers get authentic classroom discussions started? Can they teach students to do it? What are tips that can help teachers move toward full implementation of ICs? This chapter will provide some answers to these questions.

Beyond "Discussion": Indicators of Instructional Conversation (IC)

As with the other standards, the CREDE "indicators" for the Instructional Conversation standard provide benchmarks that can be used to assist teachers toward full implementation of the standard.

Instructional Conversation Indicators

For full implementation, the teacher
- arranges the classroom to accommodate conversation between the teacher and a small group of students on a regular and frequent basis;
- has a clear academic goal that guides conversation with students.
- ensures that student talk occurs at higher rates than teacher talk;
- guides conversation to include students' views, judgments, and rationales using text evidence and other substantive support;
- ensures that all students are included in the conversation according to their preferences;
- listens carefully to assess levels of students' understanding;
- assists students' learning throughout the conversation by questioning, restating, praising, encouraging, and so on; and
- guides the students to prepare a product that indicates the Instructional Conversation's goal was achieved.

In the short excerpt above, it is clear that Georgia exemplified many of these indicators. She worked in a small group, had a clear goal, and (at least during this part of the conversation) the students did more talking than she did. It is also important for teachers to make a special effort to focus on students as individuals (as Georgia does). Teachers will and should have different expectations of participation by different students. That is, some students may not feel comfortable calling out responses in a group, expecting instead to be recognized by the teacher, while other students talk in overlapping patterns, with interruption a natural part of conversation. It is important for teachers to become aware of students' differing discourse patterns learned from face-to-face interaction in their homes and communities. In this conversation, nearly all indicators were illustrated, although it is difficult to show this on the printed page. Thus, we will provide more detailed explanations on how to fully implement ICs.

Assistance Through Good Questioning

To enable authentic talk around text that contributes to meaning making, teachers use their own talk to support the development of the students' talk. This is necessary because in school, initially, children cannot perform various tasks alone and need the assistance of someone else, often the teacher (Tharp & Gallimore, 1988; Vygotsky, 1978). Scaffolding is the tool used to nudge students to do something they might not be able to do on their own. It is defined as the "process that enables a child or novice to solve a problem, carry out a task, or achieve a goal that would be beyond his unassisted efforts" (Wood, Bruner, & Ross, 1976, p. 90). Teachers scaffold students' talk through their talk (Palinscar, 1986), especially through their questioning (Tharp & Gallimore, 1988).

Benjamin Bloom (1984) created a taxonomy for categorizing the level of abstraction of questions that commonly occur in educational settings. The taxonomy provides a useful frame for teachers who are attempting to get students to think at higher levels of abstraction. The goal for ICs is to get students to answer more questions at the Comprehension, Application, and Analysis levels and fewer at the Knowledge level.

Table 7.1   Bloom's Taxonomy

Competence	*Skills Demonstrated*
Knowledge	• observation and recall of information • knowledge of dates, events, places • knowledge of major ideas • mastery of subject matter • *Question Cues:* list, define, tell, describe, identify, show, label, collect, examine, tabulate, quote, name, who, when, where, etc.
Comprehension	• understand information • grasp meaning • translate knowledge into new context • interpret facts, compare, contrast • order, group, infer causes • predict consequences • *Question Cues:* summarize, describe, interpret, contrast, predict, associate, distinguish, estimate, differentiate, discuss, extend
Application	• use information • use methods, concepts, theories in new situations • solve problems using required skills or knowledge • *Question Cues:* apply, demonstrate, calculate, complete, illustrate, show, solve, examine, modify, relate, change, classify, experiment, discover

Competence	Skills Demonstrated
Analysis	• see patterns • organize parts • recognize hidden meanings • identify components • *Question Cues:* analyze, separate, order, explain, connect, classify, arrange, divide, compare, select, explain, infer
Synthesis	• use old ideas to create new ones • generalize from given facts • relate knowledge from several areas • predict, draw conclusions • *Question Cues:* combine, integrate, modify, rearrange, substitute, plan, create, design, invent, what if?, compose, formulate, prepare, generalize, rewrite
Evaluation	• compare and discriminate between ideas • assess value of theories, presentations • make choices based on reasoned argument • verify value of evidence • recognize subjectivity • *Question Cues*: assess, decide, rank, grade, test, measure, recommend, convince, select, judge, explain, discriminate, support, conclude, compare, summarize

Think-Pair-Share Strategy

Another commonly used strategy for getting students to practice academic oral language is called Think-Pair-Share (Lyman, 1981). This strategy provides an opportunity for all students to participate in responding to the teacher's question rather than only one student at a time, as is done with traditional discourse. It allows students to mentally and orally "rehearse" their answers, which can increase the quality of student responses. When students talk over new ideas with a partner, they come to a deeper understanding of those ideas. Further, students are nearly always willing to participate when they only have to respond to a peer. It provides a safe space for English language learners who may be struggling with expressing their views and ideas.

There are many ways to implement this strategy. In the opening example in Georgia's second-grade class, Georgia used the strategy by asking the group of eight students to turn to a partner to explain the discrimination they believed the character in the book had suffered. Georgia allowed about four minutes for students to talk in pairs. Then, she invited volunteers to share with the whole group of eight. Below are standard procedures developed by Lyman (1981).

Table 7.2   Procedures for Think-Pair-Share Strategy

Activity	*Teacher Directions*
Think	The teacher poses a high-level (Bloom, 1984) question on the theme of a book or concept the class is studying and asks the students to take a minute (usually not more) to *think* about the question.
Pair	Then, the teacher invites the students to turn to someone seated near them (or to use designated partners, if desired) and discuss the answers they formed in their minds. The pairs compare responses and add to or revise their own responses based on their peer's ideas. As a pair, they come up with one response.
Share	After students talk briefly in pairs, the teacher calls for pairs to share their thinking with the rest of the class. This may lead to a larger Instructional Conversation or a listing of responses, depending on the goals of the lesson.

Examples of IC

Instructional Conversation in Middle School

As a culminating activity after completing a unit on the civil rights movement, Jayne wanted to discuss some of the information she and the students had been reading on the Web site *Voices of Civil Rights*. So she and the students reread the following excerpt from http://www.voicesofcivilrights.org/voices_story8.html.

Mexicans Had the Same Privileges and Rights as Dogs
John Raul Gutiérrez, Gillette, Wyoming

As a first-generation, Mexican American kid in Wyoming during the 1950s and 1960s, I lived in a small town where Mexicans had the same privileges and rights as dogs. Growing up, I frequently encountered signs posted on the local businesses that read "No Mexicans or Dogs Allowed." Posted signs of this nature made me feel that being of Mexican descent wasn't any better than being a mongrel that nobody wanted.

During my most impressionable years, I had a sixth-grade teacher who made no effort to hide her dislike of Mexican kids. She fostered an environment within her classroom that was not healthy or safe for Mexican American children. To her, educating a Mexican American consisted of promoting him or her whether they learned anything or not. During my final years of high school, there were local businesses where the custom of not serving Mexicans was done discreetly. I experienced not being served at restaurants, being refused entry into a barbershop, being taken in and searched by the police without cause, being frowned upon by business employees for not sitting in the customary locations or for coming into their establishments, and being called names by students and other local citizens.

On several occasions, I heard racial remarks made about my parents and family members. In regard to housing, I was refused an apartment because, as a white man explained to me, Mexicans smelled differently, and once they lived there it was impossible to clean and rent the apartment to a white person.

Jayne then asked the students to respond to the following prompt in their writer's notebooks in preparation for a discussion of this passage:

> Have things changed since the 1950s and 1960s for immigrants? Are immigrants still treated badly because of their race? Think about that and then discuss your opinion and your own experiences with that discrimination.

Jayne's goal for the upcoming conversation is evident in the writing assignment. She wanted her students to understand that the racism they sometimes see and experience is an historical pattern, and that while some progress has been made, it is an issue many people in the United States (and other countries) continue to face. Having the students write responses first allowed them to prepare their thoughts for the discussion. It is a strategy similar to Think-Pair-Share, in that it provides learners with an opportunity to organize and conceptualize ideas with words—to "rehearse" responses, in effect.

Once the students finished their writing, Jayne divided them into two groups. One group continued to work on a joint project (JPA) connected to the unit, and the other group of seven students gathered in a circle. Jayne prepared them for the IC by saying, "I want to talk a little bit about this [text] and about what you wrote. But let me say this. I want you to have a conversation with *one another*. Every time you say something, don't expect me to say something back. I really want you to talk about this with one another. Do you know what I'm saying?"

This explicit introduction into *how* to converse with one another is critical for moving away from traditional discourse. Students often need to be told that this sort of discussion will look and feel a bit different, in that students will talk with and learn from one another.

Jayne began by asking, "So, is someone willing to start the conversation?"

Marie-Ange raised her hand. "Sometime my friends treat me bad. One time I saw this one girl as we were walking into the ESL room, she started making fun of the Mexican students by calling them 'the Mexican kids, the Mexican kids,' and people around her started laughing…."

Amador said, "I think that, like, immigrants are still treated badly, but I think not as much as they were before. Like black people were slaves and now everybody has freedom, but not that much."

Miguel responded, "They have better opportunities than they did before."

Amador pondered, "And I wonder why, like, white people, like some white people are really racist, even to white people, they're racist. I mean why would they, like, be racist to immigrants if the white people are immigrants too because the United States were… Indians were here first."

Miguel followed with, "This kid that lives in my neighborhood, was like, he hated Mexicans and whenever he saw me he would say, 'Hey stupid Mexican,' and laugh."

Desiree agreed, "I think that racist people think they're better than others."

Roberto said, "I know."

Jayne wondered aloud to her students, "Do you think maybe people who are racist actually feel inferior and so they try to make themselves feel better by treating other people badly, which makes them feel more important?" The students nodded their heads and murmured in agreement.

Marie-Ange said, "Yeah, because some people, they're made fun of, so they start making fun of other people…"

Desiree added, "I don't like when I see the TV and the policemen are like hitting…."

"Like cops?" Amador asked.

"Yeah, cops are hitting Mexicans." The others murmured in agreement.

Marie-Ange added, "I was watching the History Channel about gangs, or whatever, Mexican gangs in Los Angeles. But if you like, but if you're just a Mexican on the street they try to arrest you…"

Miguel said, "I heard that Mexican and black gangs are killing each other in California."

Jayne asked, "So what do we do about this? Do you have any solutions?"

A variety of responses followed:

"I think that we're all humans and we should treat each other better."

"I'm glad we have ESL because we have friends from other cultures."

"We can learn about them."

Jayne looked to the students. "Hmm, what have you … what are some things you've learned that you've enjoyed?"

"Well, I never was in a class with black people before, and people from Mexico, and it's fun …getting to know them."

Jayne agreed. "Yeah, I think one of the best things about being, about working with ESL students is I have the privilege of working with people from all over the world, and it's really special to me."

What Jayne noticed about this Instructional Conversation was that at first students were just stating their opinions, without responding to what other students in the group were saying, but the more the conversation developed, the more they began to interact and really converse about this topic. (The "What do we do about this?" Application question from Bloom's taxonomy may be one reason.) The conversation also provided an opportunity for Jayne to find out how much her students know about what is going on in the world, which, of course, leads to future scaffolding opportunities.

By the end of this excerpt, Jayne and her students were exhibiting nearly all the IC indicators. Indeed, because the topic was so controversial, the students did not hesitate to express their opinions, and it became obvious that many of them had had experiences with racial discrimination.

Instructional Conversation With Young Children

Instructional Conversation is most difficult to conduct with young children, although teachers who have worked hard at learning it can be successful, as was Georgia with her second-grade class.

Johanna is a beginner at conducting ICs with her kindergarteners. However, we were able to capture a small-group conversation about solving problems on the playground. This conversation was part of the classroom community management program described in Chapter 3. In this conversation, Johanna and a small group of students are discussing how to deal with conflicts. She and her students exhibit some of the indicators of ICs.

Johanna begins, "OK, our problem today is, we're all at a park. And everybody wants to get on the slide at the same time. So everybody starts to try to get on the slide at that same time, and people start to get hurt. So what do you think we should do to solve our problem?"

Michele says, "Only one at a time."

Johanna repeats, "One at a time, that's a great idea! What if you are in line, and people start pushing you? How do you think you would feel, Anthony?"

Anthony cries, "Sad!"

Sam says, "Mad!"

Johanna continues, "So you might feel sad, you might feel mad. What do you think we should do if we start to feel these feelings? Juan, what do we do?"

Juan says, "Eh…put our hands on our belly…"

Johanna says, "Yes, so we're gonna put our hands on our belly to check ourselves out," and Johanna shows them how to do this. She puts her hands on her stomach and stops to think and ask herself, "How do I feel? Do I feel bad because I am hurt? Why?" This strategy is useful for very young children who may not understand why they feel bad when their feelings are hurt or when they are worried about something. It helps them identify the relationship between their emotions and their physical feelings. It also helps the English language learners because it links words with actions, another example of comprehensible input (Echevarria et al., 2004). The conversation in Johanna's classroom continues, with the students contributing suggestions for how to deal with conflicts and Johanna leading them into doing the actions suggested.

Importantly, this example is not illustrative of Instructional Conversations. Johanna still did most of the talking, and she mostly asked low-level questions. We share it because it illustrates what usually occurs as teachers begin to implement this important standard. Johanna's warmth and enthusiasm comes through, as well as her laudable goal of helping her students express their feelings. But, until the *students* do the explaining, they will not develop language skills as much as they could nor construct new understandings about the content being taught.

Another teacher with whom we have worked also attempted to develop Instructional Conversations with her second-grade class. Gayle's talk was similar to Johanna's (above), but through much coaching, Gayle was able to move beyond recitation to true IC. Gayle was leading her students toward figuring out a mystery in one of the *Nate the Great* books. A key feature of scaffolding is the gradual release of responsibility to the learner (Vygotsky, 1978). In the following example, Gayle takes a less direct role to guide the conversation than she does earlier in her lesson. She uses nonevaluative responses, more encouragement than praise, and she provides examples and suggestions (McIntyre et al., 2006). At this point in the dialogue, Gayle works with three students (Thomas, Maria, and Tyler), and she joins the group by asking a question for which she truly does not know the answer—an *authentic* question. The confusion is about a play on words involving the "case" the character is trying to solve and a "pillowcase" that becomes an important item in the story.

Gayle asks, "Pillowcase. What did he mean by that?"

Maria says, "There's a pillowcase, and he (Nate) needs to solve the *case*."

"Okay." The children begin to read, but Gayle senses confusion and asks, "Hmm? You're thinking something doesn't make sense? What doesn't make sense?"

Thomas shakes his head and says, "That doesn't make sense. *There's* the pillowcase..." (He points to the picture.)

Gayle asks, "Well, are we going by the pictures or the words? Do the words agree with the pictures? (pause) Show me the words that don't make sense." Thomas points to the words and begins to read.

After a minute, Gayle asks, "All right, what doesn't make sense?"

Maria explains, "Because it says (pause) in the beginning, Big Hex doesn't have the pillowcase."

Thomas points to the page and says, "But there it is."

Gayle looks at the page and agrees. "And there it is." (pause) "Maybe, go back to where she calls...."

Just then there is an interruption and another child joins the group. Gayle says to Thomas, "Now, explain to Tyler (who has just joined the group) what you're thinking doesn't make sense."

Thomas: "It says, on the front." As he explains, all listen intently. Finally, Tyler offers, "That's just a picture showing what it looks like."

Thomas argues, "But it says, 'Big Hex likes to play with his case.'" Thomas looks up at Tyler, eyebrows raised, and shrugs with opens palms as if to say, "How could that be?" There is a long pause while no one answers.

Gayle begins to read the text again and thinks aloud, "I think Tyler's right. I think the picture doesn't really go with the words here. It's just showing you what the pillowcase looked like."

Thomas continues the thought: "It says, one of them says, that none of them... they all have one of these (points to a picture of a pillowcase)."

Gayle says, "Yes. They all have their pillowcase."

Maria says, "I think I get it."

Thomas shouts, "I get it!"

Maria continues, "That's Big Hex. And he's chewing it and stuff. And it's just when she's washing it. It's not about the pillowcase missing. It's about *why* it's shredded."

Gayle nods and agrees, "I think it's just showing you what the pillowcase looked like."

Thomas adds, "Probably one of the cats [did the shredding]."

All three children exclaim, "Yeah, yeah!" (as in, *Now* I get it!).

Gayle says to the children, "I like the way you stopped and discussed that. That's a nice advantage of reading a book together. When you don't understand something you can say, 'Hey, Thomas, wait a minute. I don't understand this.' Bring somebody else in and help get it straight" (McIntyre et al., 2006).

In this example, Gayle releases more of the responsibility for talk to her students. Instead of highly explicit comments and directions (critical for the start of a lesson or when teaching students how to talk with one another), Gayle was just another participant trying to understand the story. Her responses include authentic questions, nonevaluative responses ("OK,""Hmm hmm"), and she uses much wait time. Indeed, there are periods of two to five seconds in which no one talks—a characteristic of real conversation and not traditional classroom discourse. In doing so, she communicates that she is expecting the children to do the majority of the talking.

Gayle also assists the meaning making when she asks the students to do the thinking when a question comes up about the meaning of the story (e.g., "What doesn't make sense?""Do the pictures agree with the words?" "What do you think?"). She also restates what children say in order to prompt them to continue to talk (e.g., "You're thinking something doesn't make sense" and "Yes, they all have their pillowcase").

Gayle also models her thinking for her students when she says, "Let me get this straight," which is a powerful tool for illustrating sense making. Perhaps the most important thing Gayle does is validate the children's contributions by incorporating them into her talk and analysis, such as when she said to Thomas, "Explain to Tyler what you're thinking doesn't make sense," and when Gayle agrees with Maria by nodding and saying, "I think it's just showing you what the pillowcase looked like." Finally, she gives credit to Tyler when she says, "I think Tyler's right," in a way that respects his thinking and does not undermine the thinking of others. She is straight with the kids and converses with them as respectful adults might do with one another. It is clear the students are constructing new understandings with their comments, such as "I think I get it."

Gayle exhibits all indicators of ICs. She clearly guides conversation to include students' views, judgments, and rationales using text evidence and other substantive support. She ensures that all students are included in the conversation according to their preferences. She listens carefully to assess levels of students' understanding and assists where necessary through questioning, restating, praising, and encouraging.

Tips for Instructional Conversations

The following lists are some reminders to teachers on their roles in Instructional Conversations adapted from McIntyre (2007). The first category (being explicit) may only be necessary for a while. Eventually students will learn how to participate in IC without the explicit talk, but it is usually necessary at first. The other three categories are always necessary.

- *Give explicit directions*
  Call for attention.
  Define concepts or words.
  Explain procedures for participation:
  1. Teach students to look at classmates and speak to them during conversation (not just to the teacher);
  2. Teach students to respond to what classmates say, not just wait their turn for their say.
  Give directions for what to think about.
  Share expectations for learning.
  Model.
  Provide examples.
  Make suggestions.

- *Cue students*
  Use emphasis when something is important.
  Remind students to speak to one another when necessary.
  Repeat or paraphrase key words or phrases.
  Use gestures for students still needing them.
  Actively listen to discern the meanings of what students are trying to say.

- *Scaffold student talk*
  Restate what the student has just said as a way to encourage.
  If students struggle, give much wait time and nod encouragingly.
  Model your own messy thinking while coming to understand something.
  Question (high-level, open-ended authentic questions).

- *Respond authentically*
  Use some nonevaluative response such as "OK" or "hmmm" as you might in normal adult conversation.
  Offer your own contribution.
  Laugh or give some other natural emotional response.
  Put students' ideas into play.
  Use much wait time.

The Instructional Conversation, like all the CREDE standards, is best conducted in concert with the other standards. That is, with any unit or sequence of lessons about any topic, teachers can include joint productive activity that is contextualized in what students already know and that also leads them into new territory that raises the level of thinking. Lessons should always provide opportunities for language learning. The Instructional Conversation is a tool for both language learning and concept learning. It also provides an opportunity for the students to illustrate what they know about the topic under study. It is a particularly useful tool when discussing complex or controversial topics that have no correct responses. But in order to have these kinds of conversations, there must be trust and respect among participants and a problem-solving atmosphere in the classroom.

Indeed, we have seen successful Instructional Conversations only in classrooms with a democratic style of teaching, in which the teacher encourages and teaches problem solving, permits student decision making, and provides much student choice, as we described in Chapter 3. These are classrooms in which there is much collaborative work and where teachers like and respect their students, as illustrated by the teachers in this book.

Assessing Your IC

The following CREDE questions can guide you to monitor your own development of ICs.

1. Do I arrange the classroom to accommodate conversation between myself and a small group of students on a regular and frequent basis?

2. Do I have a clear academic goal that guides conversation with my students?

3. Do I ensure that student talk occurs at higher rates than my own?

4. Do I guide conversation to include students' views, judgments, and rationales using text evidence and other substantive support?

5. Do I ensure that all students are included in the conversation according to their preferences?

6. Do I listen carefully to assess levels of students' understanding?

7. Do I assist students' learning throughout the conversation by questioning, restating, praising, encouraging, and so on?

8. Do I guide the students to prepare a product that indicates the Instructional Conversation's goal was achieved?

By now, it is probably apparent how these five standards work in concert. Lessons are planned, built from what students already know, and include activities for language and literacy development. They are rigorous and result in a product developed jointly. Teachers guide students in a planned conversation about what was learned in the lesson.

Teaching in this way takes time to refine. It also takes the support and involvement of students' families. Thus, our sixth principle for teaching ELLs is parent involvement, which we discuss in Chapter 8.

8

Engaging Families of English Language Learners

A Latino College Night; weekly newsletters translated for English language learners; family response journals; a multicultural fair; a "My Book" bilingual exchange; and surveys to find out how parents feel about school—each illustrates a way to reach out and engage families of English language learners. Jayne, Johanna, and other teachers in the previously mentioned Sheltered Instruction and Family Involvement (SIFI) professional development project implemented these and many other efforts. One teacher noted, "I started a coed competitive soccer team, and 90% of my team are ESL students. Their extended families often come to every game."

Why are such efforts important? What strategies and activities have teachers found to be successful in their classrooms and schools? What issues and challenges must teachers keep in mind? This chapter addresses these questions and provides many ideas for teachers seeking ways to work effectively with the families of their ELLs.

The Importance of Involving Families

A common lament of some teachers is "Some parents don't show up at school and don't respond when I try to communicate. Don't they care about their kids?" However, most parents do care and want a better life for their children than what they themselves might have experienced. Instead of not caring, many families are uncertain about how to interact with schools, don't understand how schools function, or don't feel welcome when they visit. Many ELL families may worry about becoming involved because they are not skilled at communicating their questions and concerns. Interestingly, Jayne and Johanna report that, from their experience, the parents of their ELL students often seem to put aside their insecurities and hesitations and show up for conferences and school events.

Teachers know from practical experience that students do better in school when teachers and parents are "on the same page" about what's happening in the classroom, what's expected on tests, and what's needed to support each student's learning. Knowing how to involve families who speak little or no English and have little familiarity with schooling in the United States can present a challenge for teachers. These teachers especially need ideas about how to reach out and engage students' families.

Research findings confirm what teachers know about the importance of family involvement and have demonstrated that such involvement has a positive impact on students' eventual success academically (Harvard Family Research Project, 2006/2007; Marcon, 1999; Miedel & Reynolds, 1999; Sanders & Herting, 2000). Furthermore, the benefits for students can be long-term. Barnard (2004) found that the children of low-income African-American parents who became involved with schools during the elementary years were more likely to graduate from high school than were their peers whose parents were not so connected. And, in their study of low-income, ethnically diverse children and their families, Dearing, Kreider, Simpkins, and Weiss (2006) found a predictive relationship between high levels of parental involvement and the children's eventual literacy performance.

Researchers such as Moll and González (2004) have demonstrated the benefits of getting to know families well and then building connections in teaching with families'"funds of knowledge."This concept refers to families' essential knowledge and skills needed for their effective functioning (Vélez-Ibáñez & Greenberg, 1992). For example, one family may have knowledge about carpentry, car mechanics, or quilting, while another family may know much about farming, sewing, or landscaping.

Researchers and teachers in Tuscon, Arizona, who visited and interviewed Mexican-American families subsequently developed classroom units on gardening, architecture, and more as a way to connect families' everyday use of mathematics with "school" math (Ayers, Foseca, Andrade, & Civil, 2001). Similarly, Ellen and two teachers in a rural school with a large population of poor and working class families of Appalachian descent (a minority often overlooked in the United States) developed agriculturally themed school work in reading, writing, and mathematics (McIntyre, Sweazy, & Greer, 2001). Efforts such as these enable teachers to contextualize instruction in meaningful ways, as described in Chapter 4.

The benefits of parental involvement for students' academic success seem clear from both research and practical experience. However, learning how to help more parents become involved, especially those who for a host of reasons may be less likely to participate, can be a challenge. Learning from the strategies others have tried can be a great help.

Successful Ways to Involve Families of English Language Learners

Jayne, Johanna, and others who participated in the SIFI project made a specific effort to plan and implement strategies to engage students' families, with careful attention paid to English language learners. What follows are several examples developed by the teachers that can be adapted for use in other settings.

Communicating With Families

Making sure that families get the information they need about what's going on in the classroom and school helps communicate to families that their involvement is valued. A welcoming postcard or note can start the year off with a message of interest in getting to know families and working closely with them. This can be just a simple message, such as the following note sent by fourth-grade teacher Linda to her new students.

Dear [Child's name here],
    I am very excited about meeting the children and parents of my new fourth-grade class.
    I hope you and your parents will be able to visit with me and see your new classroom at our Back to School Blast on Friday, August 12, from 4:00 to 6:00 P.M.
    Please come and celebrate the beginning of a wonderful new school year.
                        See you then!
                        Mrs. McAvinue

Starting school in such a welcoming way conveys a great deal to parents about the attitude of the school and can create the foundation for a good working relationship throughout the year. Carmen and Linda, two elementary ESL teachers who participated in the SIFI project, wrote the following reflection about their August Open House experience with the families of their ELL students.

> We worked with the bilinguals [associate instructors] to help non-English-speaking parents fill out required forms, locate bus routes and schedules, and get answers to their questions about the first weeks of school. The evening was a good positive interaction with many parents whom we already knew and a good opportunity to meet some new families. You should have seen the relief and happiness on the faces of the parents when they learned that there was bilingual help. Filling out those forms is a daunting job! We were very pleased with the relationship-building interactions of the evening.

Being able to provide translations of postcards, forms, policies, and other types of communication throughout the year is very important. For those without ready access to translators in the school, Internet Web sites now available can make translations into several languages of texts entered in English. For example, the state of Kentucky has purchased services from TransACT (www.transact .com), a Web site that provides notices and forms in several priority languages related to government mandates as well as more general topics. School districts can also post their own documents on the

Web site. Each teacher in the state has access to this resource to use in their efforts to communicate with ELL families.

Carmen and Linda used funds to purchase a year's subscription to *Home & School Connection*, a resource from Resources for Educators (www.rfeonline.com), as one strategy for communicating with the many Spanish-speaking families they worked with. Although offered only in Spanish, the newsletter is available for four grade levels. The company writes the content of the issue on topics of relevance to all students, such as homework habits, attendance, and health issues, and the school can designate its name on the front page. It arrives in the mail ready to duplicate and send home. Carmen and Linda found it to be a very helpful way to share with parents about a variety of topics as well as ideas they might try at home with their children.

One participant in the SIFI project used a Communication Log similar to the one below to document much pertinent information about communicating with families.

Table 8.1   Home School Communication Log

Communication Log						
Student Name	Parent Name	Phone Number	Date	Type Call/Visit/ Conference	Reason for Contact	Outcome

This tool became an important artifact in showing who was (and was not) contacted, what reasons initiated the contact, what type of communication took place (call, visit, or conference), and what outcomes occurred as a result of the contact with the families. The following examples from the teacher's log capture some of the phone call communications that occurred with the families:

- Call with reminder of preschool parent night.
- Call to say how well he is doing and what to do at home to help him with homework.

- Call to find out why he is sleeping in class. Mom says she will make him go to bed earlier.
- Call to remind about signing permission slip for field trip.

As these notes suggest, phone communications can help keep parents informed about upcoming events that they may have questions about or might have forgotten. And, what a great idea to make a call just to share some good news about a student! So many parents—not just those of ELLs—associate a phone call from the teacher as a sign of trouble. Changing that perception might take some time, but it is worth the effort in establishing more of a partnership relationship between school and home.

Iraida, a middle school ESL teacher, not only made an effort to communicate about the work going on in her classroom and the school but also sought the families' views about their child's experiences at school (see page 120). Although this can be a bit risky, since parents may not always be complimentary, it conveys an interest in what parents think and want and a desire to work in collaboration with them.

As important as it is, better communication is only one aspect of improving family involvement. Many teachers have also found successful ways to invite family participation in the work of the classroom.

Involving Families in Classrooms

Some ELL families might be hesitant about getting involved in their children's classrooms because they are still learning English, and others may be hesitant because of their cultural view that the role of the school is appropriately different from the role of the family. They simply may not realize that school people in the United States expect family involvement. Teachers of ELLs, then, may have to make a special effort to help families understand this view and to provide a variety of ways to encourage participation beyond the more traditional activities such as parent-teacher organizations or committees.

Johanna has developed just such a list to help her families realize that, while they may not be able to volunteer extensively in the classroom because of work schedules or other commitments, they may be able to stay involved in other ways. Take a look at her list and think of what else you might be able to add to involve families in your classroom.

What Can Teachers Have Families Do?

- Work with small groups of students
- Read to students
- Work one-on-one with a child
- Translate for students
- Help with clerical work
- Attend field trips (If a family member doesn't have a Social Security number for a criminal check, pair him/her up with his/her child and not a small group.)
- Help with dramatic performances
- Help with class parties
- Appear as a guest speaker to share traditions, dances, art forms, recipes, and so on
- Prepare materials at home
- Send in food for cooking activities
- Send in treats/prizes for treasure chest
- Record self reading a story for the listening center
- And more!

Finding out about families' interests, hobbies, talents, and work can help develop a list of resources to tap into during the year. Doing this is a way of recognizing and respecting family knowledge and connecting it to what's happening in the classroom and school. Gathering this information at the beginning of the year could take place in a brief questionnaire sent home or filled out during a parent-teacher meeting.

Johanna also elicits information from the parents of her kindergarteners as school starts. She then finds ways to involve the parents throughout the year. Here is her letter, in English and Spanish.

Dear Families,

I am writing to you for your help. I will get to spend only one year with your child, and sometimes it takes 2 or 3 months for us to get know each other well. You can help me by taking a few moments to write a letter telling me about your child. Anything you would like to share would be wonderful. You may want to tell me about your child's likes and dislikes. What are those little, special things about your child that you would like me to know? What are your child's interests? How do you think your child learns best, and what are the conditions that are most conductive to your child's success? Anything you can share with me will be confidential.

I want to know your child and I realize that no one knows a child better than his/her family. Thank you, in advance, for the opportunity to work with and get to know your child. I look forward to a full, rewarding year.

Respectfully,

Mrs. Parr

Estimadas Familias,

Le escribo a usted a pedir le ayuda. Solo tengo un año con su niño y a veces toma 2 o 3 meses para nosotros saber uno al otro bien. Usted me puede ayudar tomando unos pocos momentos de escribirme una carta que me diga acerca de su niño. Lo que usted quiciera compartir sería maravilloso. Usted me puede acerca de los aficiones y fobias del niño. ¿Qué son unas cosas especiales acerca de su niño que usted me querría dejar saber? ¿Qué son los intereses de su nino? ¿Cómo piensa usted que su niño aprende mejor y qué es las condiciones que son muy conductivas a su éxito del niño? Lo que usted puede compartir conmigo será confidencial.

Quiero conocer a su niño y se que nadie sabe a un niño mejor que su familia. Gracias, en el avance, para la oportunidad de trabajar con su niño. Espero un año repleto y remunerador.

Sinceramente,

Senora Parr

Middle school teacher Iraida also interviewed family members of her students using a "written interview" format. The following are both the English and Spanish versions.

Written Interview

I am interested in knowing your opinion about the academic behavior of your child. Please, if you would be able to complete this questionnaire, I will have a general idea about how to evaluate my work in order to improve the course for next year. You can put your name on the form or not. Thank you for your help.

1. Has your child been having a good school year?
2. Does your child like school? Explain.
3. Have you seen your child grow academically? Explain.
4. Have you seen your child grow socially? Explain.
5. Do you think your child is trying hard?
6. How do you feel about the communication between the school and home? Explain.
7. How do you feel about the homework?
8. How do you feel about the assigned projects and the home journals?

Entrevista Escrita

Estoy interesada en saber la opinión sobre el comportamiento académico de su hijo. Si usted por favor pudiera completar este cuestionario para poder tener una idea general así como evaluar mi trabajo para que sea mejor el próximo curso escolar. Usted puede poner su nombre o no. Gracias por su ayuda.

1. ¿Ha tenido su hijo un buen curso escolar? *Sí.*
2. ¿A su hijo le gusta la escuela? Explique. *Sí, se interesa por aprender cada día más.*
3. ¿Ha visto a su hijo crecer académicamente? Explique. *Sí, he visto como ella ha progresado, su aprendizaje es ascendente.*
4. ¿Ha visto a su hijo crecer socialmente? Explique. *Gradualmente, es algo tímida.*
5. ¿Usted piensa que su hijo es tratado justamente? *Sí, estoy segura.*
6. ¿Como usted se siente acerca de la comunicación entre la escuela y la casa? Explique. *Bien, siempre hay comunicación, si es necesario.*
7. ¿Como se siente acerca de la tarea de lectura? *Bien.*
8. ¿Como se siente acerca de los proyectos asignados y las tareas diarias? *Muy bien.*

Increasing Help at Home

Figuring out ways to help families become involved in supporting students' academic work at home provides another way for schools to make connections. Families want their children to succeed and may be glad to help. But, they also may lack confidence about how to provide the best kind of assistance. The "jargon" of schools ("open response," "core content," "portfolios," "standards-based units of study") can seem like a foreign language even to native English speakers!

Teachers who focus on something familiar and provide explicit guidance about what to do will usually find that families are grateful for the help and willing to do their part. Iraida found this to be true as she encouraged the parents of her students to continue their support throughout the summer. She distributed copies of simple bookmarks to her students to fill out for each book read, asking only that they record the title and author. (Others may want to add a couple of lines for students to write down what they thought of the book.) She then provided the following directions for the students and parents. [Note: This middle school has separate classes for boys and girls.]

> **Students:** Write a letter telling your parents how you will help them during the summer and how you will practice English.
>
> **Parents:** Answer your daughter's letter saying how you promise to get her to practice English and read at least three books.

The students wrote their promises of help with cleaning, cooking, and doing laundry along with reading books, watching English programs on TV, and talking in English. One even promised to "learn English fast!" The parents wrote back, mostly in Spanish, with their promises to support their children's efforts. Iraida found a simple way to convey the importance of practice at home by the students and the importance of support for that practice by the parents.

Erin, a fifth-grade teacher, engaged the families of her ELL students with a *Then and Now* book project. All ELL students, with their family's help, created a book of photos or illustrations and text to capture and contrast aspects of life in their native countries with life in their new homes in the United States. As you can see in the examples below, the students focused on the things that seemed most apparent to them.

THEN in Guatemala

NOW in the United States

THEN in China

NOW in the United States

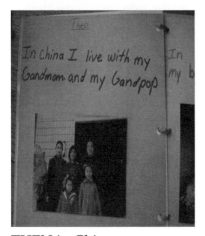

THEN in China

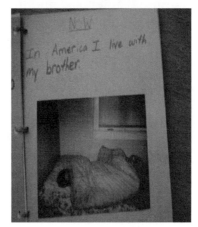

NOW in the United States

With her young kindergarteners, Johanna has already begun to establish the importance of teachers and families working together. She has used several kinds of homework ideas that involve families, such as the following:

- *Have students create a family tree, using family pictures or drawings.*

- *Create poetry notebooks.* Once a week, a new poem is placed in the notebook, and the family reads the poem with the child. One side of the notebook is in English, and the other is in their native language.
- *Prepare reading journals.* Once a week, a new book is placed in a baggie stapled to a notebook. The family reads the book together. On one side of the notebook, the child writes or draws about the book, and on the other side, the family member models how to draw and write about the book using English and/or the native language.
- *Have students create a timeline of their lives, using family pictures or drawings.*

In addition to such classroom-based ideas, many schools are exploring schoolwide ways of getting more families engaged. Workshops on topics families would find interesting and enjoyable provide one helpful approach.

Engaging Families in Workshops and Other School Events

In previous publications (Kyle, McIntyre, Miller, & Moore, 2002; Kyle, McIntyre, Miller, & Moore, 2006), Ellen, Diane and two classroom teachers offered specific details on how to plan and implement family workshops on a wide range of topics. These focused on academic-related themes of reading, mathematics, science, and social studies as well as more general ideas such as family traditions, pets, hobbies and talents, and family scrapbooks of memories. Because of the kind of topics and suggested activities, the workshops can be particularly helpful in involving ELL students and their families.

The range of topics a teacher or school can plan is almost endless and just takes the creative thinking of the school staff and parents involved. However, it also takes a perspective that engaging families in this way is not an *end* result but rather a *means* of building trust and developing effective relationships. Those relationships, in turn, can benefit students as schools and families work in closer partnership for students' academic success. A few general qualities to keep in mind about the workshops can be helpful reminders of the key purposes. Workshops should provide

- opportunities for families to share from their own experiences and knowledge;
- a focus on learning *from* as well as *with* families;
- activities that engage participants, not merely talk to them;
- a range of topics to capture families' diverse interests;
- food breaks to accommodate families' busy schedules;
- attention paid to the needs of those who struggle with reading and writing;
- attention paid to the needs of those who are learning English;
- attention paid to the needs of those with physical disabilities;
- adaptations for children with special gifts and talents;
- follow-up for those unable to attend;
- products that can be used at home and/or be displayed in the school; and
- scheduling flexibility to maximize the involvement of all families. (Kyle et al., 2006, p. 3)

In addition, teachers may find the following tips particularly useful as they take care of all the details of the workshops. Much needs to be done before, during, and after the events, and staying well organized is crucial for success.

Ideas for Family Nights

- Provide food.
- Provide transportation to and from the event for those without automobiles.
- Get ideas from families in planning the event.
- Provide child care for little ones.
- Make phone calls to encourage people to attend and nudge those you think might not come.
- Don't try to do too much in one workshop. Maintain focus.
- Have something families can take away from the workshop.
- Organize the schedule to allow for transition time.
- Stick to the schedule.
- Don't move people around too much. With a large group, this can be disastrous!
- Provide plenty of time for discussion and questions.
- Be sure to get evaluation comments.
- Provide hands-on activities (especially having adults work with their children, if they are in elementary grades).
- Tap into local resources such as community members, university people, and so on.
- Invite school board members and other community leaders.
- Get media attention.
- Take photos and deliver them to the local paper.
- Think creatively about how to get materials if funds are limited.
- Have a greeter welcome people as they arrive.
- Provide nametags. First names are fine.
- Have a sign-in sheet.
- Involve key parents as liaisons with other parents.
- Provide welcoming comments, emphasizing the importance of the event for everyone.
- Have an involved role for the principal.
- Take pictures to post in the classroom and elsewhere in the school to create interest in further workshops.
- Display work done at the workshop around the school later that week.
- Consider having a drawing for a prize at the end of the workshop and other incentives/rewards for attendance.

Ideas for Family Nights (*continued*)

- Talk up the event in the days before the workshop. Get the students excited.
- Send a reminder or call the day before or day of the workshop.
- Provide translators for ESL families.
- Tap into the resource of those families who have attended most workshops to help plan future workshops.
- Follow up with a note saying how pleased you are the families attended and provide a way for them to respond with questions or comments.
- Send materials home to those who couldn't attend.
- Take the time to reflect on the experience and record what you've learned, what worked, what didn't work, and what instructional connections can be made.
- Get started planning the next workshop! (Kyle et al., 2002, pp. 58–59)

As discussed thus far, schools can plan ways to engage families by communicating with them in varied ways, involving them in the classroom, increasing their help at home, and providing interesting and enjoyable workshops. Another approach, making visits to students' homes, can be a powerful way to get to know families, convey a desire to learn from them about their child, and establish a good working relationship. However, it's a strategy that must be planned and carried out with awareness and sensitivity.

Visiting in Students' Homes

Many teachers have found that visits to students' homes are an effective way to establish strong relationships with families and to get to know the families better than the brief encounters at school events allow. By conveying respect for families as experts about their children, teachers can learn a great deal that can then help shape instruction in meaningful ways for students. The Tucson teachers mentioned previously found this out, as have others.

For example, Gayle, a teacher of young children in a nongraded K–3 classroom, made family visits over several years as part of a research project that Ellen and Diane directed. Having learned of the families' insecurities about mathematics instruction, Gayle planned a Family Night workshop on the kind of teaching approach she was using with the students and ideas about how to help at home. Subsequently, she developed several problem-solving mathematics activities in the classroom using family-connected information she had gathered at the workshop. (For more detail, see Kyle, McIntyre, & Moore, 2001.)

Diane worked with a group of elementary teachers who chose to make family visits as a part of their professional development plan for the school year. They made visits to students' homes in late summer and then met throughout the year to talk about what they had learned and what impact the visits had had on their teaching and relationships with the families. As one teacher commented, "I knew one student had an interest in art, and I've added art in math with graphing and have an illustrator in reading groups" (Kyle, McIntyre, Sutherland, & Moore, 2005, p. 601). And another reported, "I get notes all the time telling me, 'This is way too easy,' or 'He had trouble with—,' or 'Send more of this.' It's a back-and-forth communication" (Kyle et al., 2005, p. 599).

However, this approach takes careful planning and a commitment of time not always available to teachers. Teachers must want to make such visits, must be well prepared for the experience, and must be supported by their schools if the effort is to be optimal. Those planning to make family visits are advised to follow these guidelines:

- Check your assumptions about what you expect to find.
- Keep an open mind before, during, and after the visit.
- Know that your own beliefs may be challenged.
- Go in with respect and appreciation that the family has opened their lives to you.
- View the parents/guardians as experts on their children, home, and community.
- Go in with questions, not answers. (Kyle et al., 2002, p. 62)

Once well prepared for the experience, teachers will find that making visits to students' homes results in deeper understandings, a stronger home-school partnership, and more contextualized learning experiences in the classroom.

Challenges in Involving Families

Although Johanna and Jayne and other teachers have found the above strategies to be effective ways of involving families, they have also faced many challenges in their efforts. One major issue is *time*. Many parents work long hours and some even work several jobs, thus limiting the time they can be at school as well as the time available for helping much with schoolwork at home. Even though parents may want to be involved, their economic issues can present a major barrier.

Furthermore, the time commitment for teachers must be acknowledged. Teachers, too, have family commitments and other outside-of-school responsibilities—and, yes, perhaps even second jobs! Asking teachers to spend extra time planning and putting on workshops, making visits to homes, creating new classroom activities, and so on is insensitive and unrealistic to expect without school and district resources being provided to support their efforts.

A lack of *transportation* also can limit the ability of some families to be involved. Without a car or a convenient schedule for public transportation, many families may decide that it just takes too much effort to get to their child's school unless absolutely necessary.

Another challenge can be the *funds* needed for some of the most engaging kinds of activities to involve families. Providing translated materials, food, and speakers at workshops, field trips, and other resources can strain a school's budget. Although creative minds may develop ideas about resources to be tapped, this may take some time to accomplish. Starting small may be necessary before more elaborate and more expensive plans can be implemented.

Teachers also know that a lack of *translators* can limit their ability to involve some families. While the need for Spanish-speakers may be the greatest in some communities, other communities have increasing populations of speakers of less well-known languages. Without a translator to help, many of these families may find that the effort to get involved is not beneficial and can be uncomfortable.

Despite all of the challenges, the benefits for students' success require that we make an effort to engage family, even if modest to begin with. The following tips can provide some helpful guidance.

Tips for Engaging Families

- Gather some information about what helps and/or hinders families in becoming involved at school.
- Work with others in the school about how to address the barriers families have identified.
- Work with others in the school to see how welcoming the school is and what changes are needed.
- Generate a list of many ways families could be involved, and let families know of these opportunities.
- Gather some information about families' interests, hobbies, work, and talents.
- Think of ways to connect what's learned about families with classroom instruction and other school events.
- Invite families to brainstorm new ways of engaging them in what's happening at school.
- Identify parents and other family members who would be willing to "spread the word" and get others involved.

In previous books (Kyle et al., 2002; Kyle et al., 2006), we have offered many suggestions about how to reach out to families and learn from them, as well as how to use Family Nights at school as an effective strategy for making connections. Here we again offer a few of these tips for teaching in ways that contextualize learning for students, an especially important goal when working with English language learners who are new to our country, schools, and classrooms.

Home and School: Contextualizing Instruction

- Send a survey home (translated for ELLs) or find a way to interview families in person about their interests, talents, and experiences. Include questions that elicit parents' insights about their child, such as the following: What words best describe your child? What kinds of experiences are typical of your child outside of school? What are your child's greatest interests and abilities? What goals do you have for your child? In all instances, communicate that you see the parent as the expert with knowledge that you value in teaching the child.
- Ask students to interview parents or other adults at home about interests, talents, and experiences.
- Make family visits (if possible and with careful planning) to get to know families better.

Home and School: Contextualizing Instruction *(continued)*

- Hold Family Nights to bring families together in a more informal way. Focus on academics, but build in opportunities for sharing and interaction. Consider a Family Night (after families are comfortable in attending) that highlights families' interests and expertise.
- Build into instructional units and lessons ways in which students can share what they know and be an expert about a topic.
- Invite parents or other family members to share their expertise related to an instructional topic.
- Examine your typical homework assignments to see if they tap into your students' experiences or could be redesigned to do so.
- Find ways during teaching to make incidental connections with students' lives outside of school.

Assessing Your Family Involvement

There are no CREDE questions to pose for assessing your family involvement. However, we believe that assessing your involvement of families is worth is worth doing to ensure that all your students' families are connected to the school and you with them. We suggest the following questions:

1. Do I know anything about the families of each of my students?

2. How many of my students' family members have I met?

3. How flexible are my homework policies?

4. How do my homework policies connect with students' home knowledge?

5. How invitational have I been with my students' families? How much have I communicated that I want to know them, enlist their support, and see them in the school and community?

6. How comfortable are the families in and around the school?

7. Have I reached out to the families enough?

Self assessment of this sort can lead teachers on their way to developing the kind of positive relationships necessary for strong family support and accelerated student achievement.

9

Teaching English Language Learners in All Classrooms

In today's schools, all teachers can and must see themselves as teachers of English language learners. Teachers in self-contained ESL or ELL classrooms must teach content along with language, and teachers in mainstream classrooms must teach English language oral and written skills while they teach the content. Indeed, mainstream classroom teachers are essential for the success of our immigrant population and other English language learners. Yet, many teachers faced with teaching ELLs have not had the training or professional development necessary for feeling confident and being successful with teaching them. Accomplishing this is no small feat and will require the best efforts of educators. In this last chapter, we offer a few suggestions about the work that is needed by all of us.

Beyond a "Model" Approach

The standards for effective teaching developed by CREDE researchers and described in teachers' practices throughout this book require more than learning about how to implement a new "model" in the classroom. Certainly, teachers can learn a great deal from reading about how others have developed joint productive activities with their students, contextualized learning with connections to students' past experiences, focused on language and literacy across content areas, maintained high standards in a rigorous curriculum, and engaged students in meaningful instructional conversations. After all, if we didn't believe that teachers could learn from their peers, we would never have written this book so full of classroom vignettes.

However, we also know a lot about the teachers who have contributed their work to these pages. They are excellent teachers with a well-grounded sociocultural perspective on teaching, who not only value the diversity of students in their classrooms but also understand how to implement effective instructional practices for them. In other words, learning about the CREDE standards and their application and, more specifically, about modifications for ELLs has been consistent with their already established practice. This is not to say that they haven't had to "stretch" as they have tried out new ideas. Indeed, they have appropriately been in their zone of proximal development (ZPD; Vygotsky, 1978) as they have learned. But, they have had a strong foundation from which to build. Other teachers, though, have had more of a struggle. Attempting to learn a new approach without a compatible theoretical view or the skills needed to apply the strategies in practice has made their attempt more difficult.

Tharp et al., (2000) have provided much detail about the necessary conditions—both philosophical and practical—needed in order to create classrooms within which the CREDE standards can flourish. You may have felt overwhelmed by some of the teaching examples, especially those that involved simultaneous, small-group, joint productive activity that occurred in learning centers, such as in Justin's high school classroom presented in Chapter 5. Justin was able to accomplish this instructional environment after developing beliefs about how students learn alongside his development of specific principles and strategies for carrying out those beliefs. Similarly, Tharp et al. (2000) suggest that "simultaneous activities involving a variety of roles, abilities, and interactions, all imbued with a consistent set of values (p. 143)" must be in place. Realizing that creating such classrooms takes time, they outline a five-phase process, with each having descriptions of teacher and student roles, grouping arrangements, and work to be accomplished. This phasing in takes place over several weeks of focused effort and reflection.

We encourage those interested in exploring more fully the ideas we have presented in this book to reflect first on such questions as these: (1) How compatible are these suggestions with my views about "good teaching"? (2) Which of the CREDE principles would be the easiest for me to use in my classroom, and which would take some time to develop? (3) What are some potential barriers and challenges that I need to be aware of and attempt to resolve? Because our professional development projects related to these standards included research studies on teachers' development of the standards and of sheltered instruction for English language learners, we will respond to the above questions with information gleaned from those studies.

Compatible Views

When we assessed teachers' development (McIntyre et al., 2007) on the implementation of sheltered instruction over a year or more, we found that those teachers most successful at fully implementing sheltered instruction were those who enthusiastically and repeatedly reported to us during the professional development sessions, "Well, this is just good teaching!" We had said the same thing ourselves more than once. But we have also come to believe that the principles we espouse above are "good teaching PLUS"; that is, the fundamentals about how children learn are foundational to the principles. Yet, the indicators of each of the standards provide an additional layer of refinement toward excellent teaching. The extra explicitness, a focus on both language and content, and product-driven tasks seem to nudge teachers toward a more refined implementation of good teaching.

We also found that the most successful teachers were those who generally liked students and valued the contributions that English language learners and their families brought to the classroom and U.S. society. We heard positive and enthusiastic comments about the students by these successful teachers. The teachers saw *themselves* (rather than the students, parents, society, or some other entity) as the key to students' academic success. These were also teachers open to learning and changing.

Development of CREDE Standards

The first two authors of this book (Ellen and Diane) have worked with teachers on the development of the CREDE standards for more than a decade. Most of the teachers with whom we have worked find the standard *Contextualization* the easiest and most sensible way to begin to focus on the implementation of these standards. Teachers have long heard about the importance of students' prior knowledge and building from what they know. Contextualization is just that, with a focus not just on what students know from family, previous lessons, and peer interactions but also on the linguistic patterns in their first language and cultural norms on how to interact. Knowing the different ways students communicate comfortably is important for helping students to feel safe in the classroom and willing to make academic efforts. For teachers, this means not only getting to know students well inside and outside of school but also observing them and listening to them carefully to see how they communicate (e.g., Do they use eye contact, overlap their speech, speak up in class or wait until after class?).

Teachers also find the standard of *Developing Language and Literacy* to be a starting point. Many teachers have always heard the phrase "All teachers are teachers of reading" and have understood that they teach students, not content. That is, they put the needs of students before the need to cover a curriculum. And so, if a teacher finds that her students do not write well, she teaches them to improve their writing through learning the content, as we saw with teachers in Chapters 3 and 5. If high-school-content teachers have English language learners who need practice with oral language, they can provide that time through activities like "Think-Pair-Share" described in Chapter 5. These are sometimes simple instructional moves that can make huge differences, and the teachers we have studied have found numerous ways to do this. One simple resource that helps build oral language and literacy skills, often through joint productive activity, is *Tools for Teaching Content Literacy* by Janet Allen (2004).

Most teachers also have some familiarity with *Joint Productive Activity* (JPA) through training in cooperative learning or something similar. However, this standard is not as easily implemented as the above two, often because fully implemented JPA involves more than group work or even cooperative learning. First, the focus is on product, not process, although process is important. Second, teachers and students plan together the work they will do and the products they will accomplish. The teacher participates in the JPA, offering ideas, suggestions, and even answers to questions when appropriate. The teacher is a co-learner with the student, whenever possible. This makes group work more like an apprentice model of teaching/learning, characteristic of the Vygotskian theory we espoused in Chapters 1 and 2. Thus, in implementing JPA, as with all the standards, attention to the indicators bulleted in each chapter is essential.

Rigorous Curriculum and *Instructional Conversation* are often the two standards most difficult to implement. To maintain a rigorous curriculum, teachers must not only know the content they teach very well but also understand developmental milestones in the acquisition of that content. Indeed, when a student acquires a new skill or concept, the teacher must anticipate what is appropriate for the student to learn next. Well-researched textbooks are a tool for moving to the next step, but they do not always correspond to the appropriate skills students should acquire. Finally, the teacher must know what students know; she or he must be aware of the developmental skills and concepts in order to teach just beyond what the students know, making flexible small groups critical for differentiating the curriculum.

The *Instructional Conversation* (IC) is the primary tool for implementing all the standards. Importantly, it is not simply "discussion." Discussion in traditional teaching nearly always means that the teacher does most of the talking, with students only responding to questions asked by the teacher. Nor are ICs simply good conversations about books, however valuable that might be. ICs are planned discussions that lead students to new understandings about content, and they are very hard to accomplish. But when teachers learn to lead these kinds of conversations, they often see dramatic learning in students: that famous "light bulb" will go on for one or more students in nearly every IC. Seeing students learn becomes a regular thing, not an occasional, this-makes-it-all-worth-it moment.

Barriers and Challenges

Some of the teachers in our studies were less successful at implementing the standards, not because of something within themselves but because of situations over which they had little control. Most of these factors had nothing to do with students! For example, when some teachers in a building were attempting to change their teaching to reflect the standards while other teachers were implementing traditional instruction with no intentions for change, change was difficult. Teachers need the support of their peers for morale, materials, and motivation. They need assistance with reflecting on why teaching goes well or flops. Further, teachers need support from the leadership in their building. A principal or lead teacher needs to know about and respect what the teacher is attempting to do if the teacher is to have success.

One barrier to full implementation of the standards may be the materials and textbooks adopted by the school or district. If the materials are varied and include more than printed materials, and if teachers are permitted to use them flexibly, then teachers will be more free to implement these standards. If teachers must strictly adhere to materials and follow the curriculum in a strict sequence, it will be more difficult. If teachers must implement a scripted curriculum, then it will be impossible to implement the five CREDE standards.

Preparation of Teachers and Teacher Educators

The Sheltered Instruction and Family Involvement (SIFI) project that led to the development of this book provided a professional development experience for practicing teachers. As we noted previously, the vast majority of teachers in today's classrooms have not been prepared to teach the many English language learners who are now students in U.S. schools and whose numbers are likely to increase. These teachers need professional development opportunities to expand their understandings about ELLs and about the most effective instructional strategies for teaching them the content they need to acquire while they are also learning to speak, read, and write in English.

Such professional development for teachers could be provided by school districts, school-based resource teachers, or universities—or as a collaboration among all of these providers in a well-designed initiative to address this need. Guskey (2002) and August and Shanahan (2006b) have pointed out the characteristics of excellent professional development that makes a difference in teachers' practices. During such experiences, teachers are able to apply what they learn directly to their teaching, continue to use their established curriculum materials, and relate their instruction to the district and state academic standards that guide their work. Addressing more specifically the kind of professional development most effective for focusing on instruction for language minority students, August and Shanahan (2006b) noted that it usually includes meetings, workshops, follow-up, opportunities for hands-on practice, and facilitation by outside collaborators. Further, long-term projects usually succeed more than short-term projects do, although what is taught and how it is taught matters most.

The continued learning of teachers currently in classrooms, then, must be addressed and addressed well. But, what about the preparation of preservice teachers? If teacher education programs do not include specific and detailed instruction on how future elementary, middle, and secondary teachers can accommodate the needs of ELLs, then the situation in today's classrooms will not improve for these students. They will continue to fail to learn the content knowledge needed for academic success. This, however, raises a related question: How many teacher education professors who explain methods of teaching mathematics, science, social studies, and language arts know about effective instructional strategies for teaching ELLs or how to differentiate instruction to meet their needs? Unless teacher educators engage in professional development on this topic and expand their own knowledge and skills, they will be little able to prepare future teachers for the students waiting for them in their classrooms.

Concluding Remarks

In a recent interview with students of one of the teachers in the SIFI project, one student observed, "Sometimes American [non-SIFI] teachers explain us [only] a little, but they don't understand that we are not like the others that speak English really good so she [the American teacher] explains really fast. And we say, like, can you say that again? And she get mad." But about the teacher who participated in the SIFI project, the student noted, "She explain us like with the time that we need and explain slowly with easy words."

This ELL student has the advantage of working with a teacher who has learned the kinds of instructional strategies most likely to be beneficial for ELLs. As a result, this student's potential is greater for academic success and future productive citizenship. Our hope is that all ELL students in the United States may one day be as fortunate.

References

Allen, J. (2004). *Tools for teaching content literacy*. Portland, ME: Stenhouse Publishers.

Almasi, J. (1995). The nature of fourth graders' sociocognitive conflicts in peer-led and teacher-led discussions of literature. *Reading Research Quarterly, 30*, 314–335.

August, D., & Erikson, F. (2006). Qualitative studies of classroom and school practices. In D. August & T. Shanahan (Eds.), *Developing literacy in second-language learners: Report of the National Literacy Panel on Language-Minority Children and Youth* (pp. 489–522). Mahwah, NJ: Lawrence Erlbaum Associates.

August, D., & Shanahan, T. (Eds.). (2006a). *Developing literacy in second-language learners: Report of the National Literacy Panel on Language-Minority Children and Youth*. Mahwah, NJ: Lawrence Erlbaum Associates.

August, D., & Shanahan, T. (2006b). Synthesis: Instruction and professional development. In D. August & T. Shanahan (Eds.), *Developing literacy in second-language learners: Report of the National Literacy Panel on Language-Minority Children and Youth* (pp. 53–74). Mahwah, NJ: Lawrence Erlbaum Associates.

Ayers, T., Foseca, A., Andrade, R., & Civil, M. (2001). Creating learning communities: The "build your dream house" unit. In E. McIntyre, A. Rosebery, & N. González (Eds.), *Classroom diversity: Connecting curricula to students' lives* (pp. 92–99). Portsmouth, NH: Heinemann Educational Books.

Barnard, W. (2004). Parent involvement in elementary school and educational attainment. *Children & Youth Services Review, 26*(1), 39–62.

Beers, K. (2002). *When kids can't read: What teachers can do*. Portsmouth, NH: Heinemann Educational Books.

Billings, L., & Fitzgerald, J. (2002). Dialogic discussion and the Paideia seminar. *American Educational Research Journal, 39*, 907–941.

Bloom, B. S. (1984). *Taxonomy of educational objectives*. Boston: Allyn & Bacon.

Brown, H. D. (2000). *Principles of language learning and teaching* (4th ed.). White Plains, NY: Longman, Inc.

Cazden, C. (1988). *Classroom discourse: The language of teaching and learning*. Portsmouth, NH: Heinemann Educational Books.

Champs: *A Proactive and Positive Approach to Classroom Management* (Sprick, Garrison, & Howard, 1998).

Chen, C., Kyle, D. W., & McIntyre, E. (2008). Helping teachers work effectively with English learners and their families. *School Community Journal 18*(1), 7–20.

Coles, R. (2004). *The story of Ruby Bridges*. New York: Scholastic Books.

Corder, S. P. (1973). *Introducing applied linguistics.* Harmondsworth, UK: Penguin Books.

Cummins, J. (1979). Cognitive/academic language proficiency, linguistic interdependence, the optimal age question and some other matters. *Working Papers on Bilingualism, 19,* 197–205.

Cummins, J. (2003). BICS and CALP: Origins and rationale for the distinction. In C. B. Paulston & G. R. Tucker (Eds.), *Sociolinguistics: The essential readings* (pp. 322–328). London: Blackwell.

Da Costa, T. A. (2000). How writing helps me. In A. Desetta and S. Wolin (Eds.), *The struggle to be strong* (pp. 112–114). Minneapolis, MN: Free Spirit Publishing, Inc.

Dalton, S. S. (2007). *Five standards for effective teaching: How to succeed with all learners.* San Francisco: Jossey-Bass.

Dearing, E., Kreider, H., Simpkins, S., & Weiss, H. (2006). Family involvement in school and low-income children's literacy performance: Longitudinal associations between and within families. *Journal of Educational Psychology, 98,* 653–664.

Delpit, L. D. (1995). *Other people's children; Cultural conflict in the classroom.* New York: The New Press.

de Paola, T. (1979). *Oliver Button is a sissy.* Fort Worth, TX: Voyager Books.

Echevarria, J., Vogt, M. E., & Short, D. (2004). *Making content comprehensible for English language learners: The SIOP model* (2nd ed.). Boston: Pearson.

Ferguson, R. F. (1998). Teachers' perceptions and expectations and the black-white test score gap. In C. Jencks & M. Phillips (Eds.), *The black-white test score gap* (pp. 273–317). Washington, DC: Brookings Institution Press.

Finn, P. J. (1999). *Literacy with an attitude: Educating working-class children in their own self-interest.* New York: SUNY Press.

Foster, M., & Peele, T. B. (2001). Ring my bell: Contextualizing home and school in an African American community. In E. McIntyre, A. Rosebery, & N. González (Eds.), *Classroom diversity: Connecting curriculum to students' lives.* Portsmouth, NH: Heinemann Educational Books.

Freeman, Y. S., & Freeman, D. E. (2002). *Closing the achievement gap: How to reach limited-formal-schooling and long-term English learners.* Portsmouth, NH: Heinemann.

Gay, G. (2002). Preparing for culturally responsive teaching. *Journal of Teacher Education, 53,* 106–116.

Goldenberg, C. (1993). Instructional conversations: Promoting comprehension through discussion. *The Reading Teacher, 46,* 316–326.

Guskey, T. R. (2002). Does it make a difference? Evaluating professional development. *Educational Leadership, 59*(6), 45–51.

Harvard Family Research Project. (2006/2007). *Family involvement in elementary school children's education.* Cambridge, MA: Harvard Family Research Project, Harvard Graduate School of Education.

Johnson, A., & Beck, B. (2007). *Just like Josh Gibson.* New York: Aladdin Books.

Kentucky Department of Education. (2008). *Kentucky writing handbook.* Retrieved March 28, 2008, from http://www.education.ky.gov/KDE/ Instructional +Resources/High+School/English+Language+Arts/ Writing/Kentucky +Writing+Handbook.htm

Krashen, S. D. (1981). *Principles and practice in second language acquisition. English language teaching series.* London: Prentice-Hall International (UK) Ltd.

Krashen, S. D. (1990). Bilingual education and second language acquisition theory. In Office of Bilingual Bicultural Education (Ed.), *Schooling and language minority students: A theoretical framework* (14th ed., pp. 51–79). Sacramento, CA: Evaluation, Dissemination and Assessment Center, California State University.

Kyle, D., McIntyre, E., Miller, K., & Moore, G. (2002). *Reaching out: A K–8 resource for connecting families and schools.* Thousand Oaks, CA: Corwin Press.

Kyle, D., McIntyre, E., Miller, K., & Moore, G. (2006). *Bridging school & home through family nights.* Thousand Oaks, CA: Corwin Press.

Kyle, D., McIntyre, E., & Moore, G. (2001). Connecting mathematics instruction with the families of young children. *Teaching Children Mathematics, 8*(2), 80–86.

Kyle, D., McIntyre, E., Sutherland, M., & Moore, G. (2005). Making family visits as a school-wide effort: Strategies, benefits, and challenges. In R. Martinez-Gonzalez, M. Perez-Herrero, & B. Rodriguez-Ruiz (Eds.), *Family-school-community partnerships: Merging into social development* (pp. 587–610). Oviedo, Spain: Publica Grupo SM.

Ladson-Billings, G. (2008). *The dreamkeepers: Successful teachers of African American children* volume 18 (1), 7-20. San Francisco: Jossey-Bass.

Lensmire, T. (1994). *When children write: Critical re-visions of the writing workshop.* New York: Teachers College Press.

Lesaux, N.K., Koda, K., Siegel, L.S., & Shanahan, T. (2006). Development of literacy. In D. August & T. Shanahan (Eds.), *Developing literacy in second-language learners: Report of the National Literacy Panel on Language-Minority Children and Youth* (pp. 75–122). Mahwah, NJ: Lawrence Erlbaum Associates.

Lewis, C. (1997). The social drama of literature discussions in a fifth/sixth grade classroom. *Research in the Teaching of English, 31,* 205–239.

Lozanov, G. (1979). *Suggestology and Outlines of Suggestopedy.* New York: Gordon and Breach Science Publishers.

Lyman, F. (1981). Think-pair-share. Retrieved June 18, 2008, from http://www.readingquest.org/strat/tps.html

Many, J. E. (2002). An exhibition and analysis of verbal tapestries: Understanding how scaffolding is woven into the fabric of instructional conversations. *Reading Research Quarterly, 37,* 376–407.

Marcon, R. (1999). Positive relationships between parent school involvement and public school inner-city preschoolers' development and academic performance. *School Psychology Review, 28*(3), 395–412.

McIntyre, E. (2007). Story discussion in the primary grades: Balancing authenticity and explicit teaching. *The Reading Teacher, 60*(7), 610–620.

McIntyre, E., Kyle, D. W., & Chen, C. (2007, April). *Teacher learning of sheltered instruction and family involvement.* Paper presented at the annual meeting of the American Educational Research Association, Chicago.

McIntyre, E., Kyle, D. W., & Moore, G. (2006). A teacher's guidance toward small-group dialogue in a low-SES primary grade classroom. *Reading Research Quarterly, 41*(1), 36–63.

McIntyre, E., Kyle, D. W., Munoz, M., Chen, C., & Beldon, S. (2008, March). *Student learning in sheltered instruction classrooms.* Paper presented at the annual meeting of the American Educational Research Association, New York.

McIntyre, E., Rosebery, A., & González, N. (2001). *Classroom diversity: Connecting curricula to students' lives.* Portsmouth, NH: Heinemann Educational Books.

McIntyre, E., Sweazy, R. A., & Greer, S. (2001). Agricultural field day: Linking rural cultures to school lessons. In E. McIntyre, A. Rosebery, & N. González (Eds.), *Classroom diversity: Connecting curricula to students' lives.* (pp. 76–84). Portsmouth, NH: Heinemann Educational Books.

Miedel, W., & Reynolds, A. (1999). Parent involvement in early intervention for disadvantaged children: Does it matter? *Journal of School Psychology, 37*(4), 379–402.

Miller, M. (1990). *Who uses this?* New York: Scholastic Books.

Moll, L., & González, N. (2004). Engaging life: A funds-of-knowledge approach to multicultural education. In J. Banks (Ed.), *Handbook of research on multicultural education* (pp. 699–715). San Francisco: Jossey-Bass.

Moll, L. C. (1992). Bilingual classroom studies and community analysis. *Educational Researcher, 21,* 20–24.

Myers, W. D. (1989). *Fallen angels.* New York, NY: Scholastic Books.

National Institute of Child Health and Human Development (NICHD). (2000). *Teaching children to read: An evidence-based assessment of the scientific research literature on reading and its implications for reading instruction* (Report of the National Reading Panel). Washington, DC: Author.

Nieto, S. (1999). *The light in their eyes: Creating multicultural learning communities.* New York: Teachers College Press.

Palinscar, A. S. (1986). The role of dialogue in providing scaffolded instruction. *Educational Psychologist, 21,* 73–98.

Roehler, L., & Duffy, G. (1991). Teachers' instructional actions. In R. Barr, M. L. Kamil, P. Mosthenthal, & P. D. Pearson (Eds.), *Handbook of reading research* (Vol. II, pp. 861–884). Mahwah, NJ: Lawrence Erlbaum Associates.

Rogoff, B. (1990). *Apprenticeship in thinking: Cognitive development in social context.* New York: Oxford University Press.

Rosenthal, N. (1995). *Speaking of reading.* Portsmouth, NH: Heinemann.

Ryan, P. M. (2002). *Esperanza rising.* New York: Blue Sky Press.

Sanders, M., & Herting, J. (2000). Gender and the effects of school, family, and church support on the academic achievement of African-American urban adolescents. In M. G. Sanders (Ed.), *Schooling students placed at risk: Research, policy, and practice in the education of poor and minority adolescents* (pp. 141–161). Mahwah, NJ: Lawrence Erlbaum Associates.

Saunders, W. M. & Goldenberg, C. (1999). *The effects of instructional conversations and literature logs on the story comprehension and thematic understanding of English proficient and limited English proficient students.* Santa Cruz, CA: Center for Research on Education, Diversity, and Excellence.

Scraper, K. (2005). *Maya Lin linking people and places.* Boston: Celebration Press.

Sprick, R., Garrison, M., & Howard, L. (1998). *CHAMPS: A proactive and positive approach to classroom management.* Eugene, OR: Pacific Northwest Publishing.

Tharp, R. G., & Dalton, S. S. (2007). Orthodoxy, cultural compatibility, and universals in education. *Comparative Education, 43,* 53–70.

Tharp, R. G., Estrada, P., Dalton, S. S., & Yamauchi, L. A. (2000). *Teaching transformed: Achieving excellence, fairness, inclusion, and harmony.* Boulder, CO: Westview Press.

Tharp, R. G., & Gallimore, R. (1988). *Rousing minds to life: Teaching, learning, and schooling in social context.* New York: Cambridge University Press.

Vaughan, J., and Estes, T. (1986). *Reading and reason beyond the primary grades.* Boston: Allyn & Bacon.

Vélez-Ibáñez, C., & Greenberg, J. (1992). Formation and transformation of funds of knowledge among U.S. Mexican households. *Anthropology and Education Quarterly, 23,* 313–335.

Vygotsky, L. S. (1978). *Mind in society: The development of higher psychological processes.* Cambridge: Harvard University Press.

Wood, P., Bruner, J., & Ross, G. (1976). The role of tutoring in problem solving. *Journal of Child Psychology and Psychiatry, 17,* 89–100.

Index